BUTTONS

BUTTONS

DIANA EPSTEIN • MILLICENT SAFRO

FOREWORD BY JIM DINE • PREFACE BY TOM WOLFE

PHOTOGRAPHY BY JOHN PARNELL

HARRY N. ABRAMS, INC., PUBLISHERS

Editor: MARK GREENBERG

Designer: CAROL ANN ROBSON

A NOTE ON THE PHOTOGRAPHY

Most of the buttons included in this book are pictured at their actual size; in those cases where they are enlarged in order to show details of imagery or workmanship, however, this has been indicated.

Library of Congress Cataloging-in-Publication Data

Epstein, Diana.
Buttons / Diana Epstein, Millicent Safro
photography by John Parnell.
p.   cm.
Includes bibliographical references (p.   ) and index.
ISBN 0–8109–3113–3
1. Buttons—Catalogs.   2. Epstein, Diana—Art collections—
Catalogs.   3. Safro, Millicent, 1934–   —Art collections—
Catalogs.   4. Buttons—Private collections—New York (N.Y.)—
Catalogs.   I. Safro, Millicent, 1934–   II. Title.
NK3668.5.E665   1991
646'.19—dc20
90–24272
CIP

Page 1: Metal and glass, various countries, late 19th to early 20th century "Gay Nineties," or "Victorian jewels," are collectors' terms for these jeweled coat or cloak buttons, and they probably refer as much to a nostalgic vision of the period in which they were made, between 1890 and 1920, as to any quality specific to the buttons. Ornate borders and the prominent central "stones," which, in fact, are glass, are characteristic of this type, no doubt because they evoke the extravagance and excess associated with fin-de-siècle society. Most of these buttons were made in France, although a number have been found with German maker's marks. *Page 2: Various materials, 18th and 19th centuries* Functionalism bows to visual fantasy in this impossibly bedazzling collection of buttons. *Page 3: Porcelain, various countries, mid-19th century* The metal rims and size make these otherwise simple calico buttons extremely scarce. *Page 5: Mosaic, Italian, late 19th century* These four buttons are Italian micromosaics made of minute pieces of colored glass ("tesserae"), with red and green glass borders that simulate semiprecious stones. As the nineteenth century progressed, classical motifs, such as the picturesque gold-mounted ruins at bottom, gave way to more humble scenes of pets and peasants. Mosaic buttons were made by Roman craftsmen trained in the Vatican workshops and were produced as souvenirs. *Page 6: Ceramic, American, early to mid-19th century* These uniquely American ceramic buttons are believed to have come from several potteries that flourished in Connecticut in the early to mid-nineteenth century. The variegated buttons with green and lighter brown tints on the left side of the large four-hole button at center are examples known to have been produced by these potteries. The streaked and mottled darker brown shades, on the upper right and lower center, are typically known as Rockingham glaze (after the brown lead glazes developed by the Rockingham kiln in England). Larger household items with these glazes represent an area of familiar and important collectible Americana. It is refreshing and surprising to find the same palette of brown glazes, in miniature form, on a great variety of buttons of the period. *Page 7: Reverse painting, French, ca. 1860* These unusual underglass buttons were made by the prominent French button company Albert Parent et Cie. The glittery effect is created by ground abalone shell, which shows through the unpainted portions of the design; the wolf's head is especially rare.

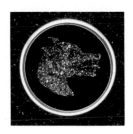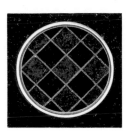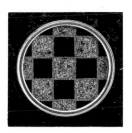

CONTENTS

To the Memories of
Zachary Stewart and Joseph Healy

Acknowledgments

In making this book, we are grateful to many people for their contributions and encouragement. We even thank each other for inspiring confidence, sharing the work, and giving support.

Our profound appreciation and thanks go first to Nina Rosenblatt, whose research, insights, and contributions throughout the book were of incalculable worth. We thank Carla Tscherny and Mary Elizabeth Mitchell for their early assistance and enthusiasm.

We extend terrific applause to our right- and left-hand men, Deborah Hanson and Susan Morgenstern, whose endless labor has made order and logic out of the chaos of countless details. Sincere thanks and appreciation for their daily and invaluable help also go to David Gibilie, Barbara Stoj, Melissa Zexter, and Shawn Kimber.

We are enormously indebted to our editor, Mark Greenberg, for his expertise, astute judgment, and generous assistance throughout the project. We are grateful that he conceived and believed in the idea of making a book about buttons.

We owe particular thanks to John Parnell for his untiring attention to detail and the care he took in photographing small objects with great respect, and to Carol Robson for designing the book with exceptional sensitivity and aesthetic sense.

Very special thanks are due to our good friend Lenore Tawney for her constant encouragement and support; her courageous attitude, always say "do it," makes her the heroine of our book.

We thank our families and friends, whose understanding and affection have been more than helpful during the time when we disengaged from society in order to focus on the history of buttons.

Finally, any effort to investigate and write about an obscure subject such as buttons must be based on the work of others. We heartily thank the collectors and authors who so generously shared their findings.

DIANA EPSTEIN • MILLICENT SAFRO

Foreword
by Jim Dine

I have always sewn on my own buttons. My grandfather taught me and I would improvise. I am forever changing the buttons on my clothes, usually for the same reason that I correct a drawing or shift colors around in my paintings: it sharpens the total effect and creates harmony.

When I first visited Tender Buttons, Diana Epstein and Millicent Safro's shop, twenty years ago, I experienced the sensation of being in familiar territory, like the bottom of my mother's sewing basket or Joseph Cornell's workshop. This tiny repository was chock-full of buttons in lovely, neat rows. There were usually three sizes of each kind in gray boxes—equivalents of the classic brown-paper bag. There were also bits of furniture, the kind so favored in the late fifties and early sixties by Upper East Side bohemians: Bentwood chairs by Thonet and wonderful, odd vitrines from old shops all over America.

With a connoisseur's eye and a canny sense of small-town shopkeeping, these women have created a shrine to buttons. Diana's handwriting on each box is plain and beautiful and bespeaks the love of penmanship that people of my generation were taught. There are framed collections of buttons in series, or buttons that relate to each other because they are all mother-of-pearl or scrimshaw—married because these two experts' eyes said they belong together. They've taught me how moving the plain brown or black four-hole button can be by insisting that it is far more lasting and, therefore, important than fancy Japanese ivory ones or silver studs from Taxco in the forties.

One day I was finally asked upstairs into their Ali Baba's cave. There the plain and the rare, the odd and the ugly are catalogued and pasted on cards side by side with the "home runs," which include a button from the eighteenth century that is paper under glass with a fine pencil landscape drawing, minute Italian mosaics of the Seven Wonders of the World, and sad, old, historic tartans.

These button keepers never cease to produce some object, expensive or poor, that charms my old seamstress's soul. I love them for that.

PREFACE
BY TOM WOLFE

The screening room went dark, the curtain parted with a sound like a model train on a track, and ninety-some other souls and myself settled back for the movie version of Thomas Mann's *Death in Venice*. Artfully, artfully, lugubriously, lugubriously, we were drawn deeper, deeper into Mann's swamp of turn-of-the-century decadence. Venice . . . 1911 . . . the Steamer Trunk Set converges from all over Europe upon the Lido for the height of the resort season . . . the great German novelist, Gustave von Aschenbach, played by Dirk Bogarde, arrives in a gondola that looks oddly like a coffin . . . not knowing he is about to meet an invisible intruder, death, in the form of a plague that seeps through Venice like the red death in Poe's "Masque of the Red Death" . . . soon realizing he should flee but remaining riveted to this rich, ripe, rotting Adriatic resort by his passion for a stranger, Tadzio, a beautiful fourteen-year-old high-bourgeois Polish boy . . . leading to the climactic evening on which von Aschenbach sits in the darkness on the hotel veranda staring with the most deadly longing at Tadzio, who stands nearby wearing a navy-blue military-style tunic with a row of gold buttons running from his neck to below his waist . . . A close-up of von Aschenbach's face . . . What is it we see in that desperate stare? A pedophiliac yearning? A longing for lost youth? For lost innocence? For ecstasy and death? For Eros and Thanatos in one? For a civilization once sublimely beautiful and now hopelessly decayed?

The screening room was so silent, so still, you could feel the colon pulses of the digital watch on your wrist. Just then, from out of the darkness, came the unmistakable contralto stage whisper of the wife of one of New York's best-known dress designers:

"Look, Darling! Those *buttons!* To *die!*"

Bango. That did it. The air went out of Thomas Mann's götterdämmerungische angst, just like that. Not all the Nobel novelists and Dirk Bogardes in the world were going to pump it back up, either, not that night, not for that audience. Scores walked out of the screening room exhaling between clenched teeth the New York Sigh, the heat-seeking sigh that aims to slay.

But as Ed Koch said constantly, hopelessly, in his last year as mayor of New York: "Isn't the truth relevant?" After all, *Death in Venice* is a movie in which von Aschenbach's motives are, if anything, murkier than Hamlet's. Which of us could say for certain that he longed for anything other than . . . a set of gold buttons like that nice-looking lad's?

As you will learn in the pages that follow, he would not have been the first to lose himself, if not his soul, to an obsession with buttons. William Blake offered to let you "see a world in a grain of sand" and "hold infinity in the palm of your hand." Diana Epstein and Millicent Safro are about to do that much for you with buttons.

The Mesdames Epstein and Safro themselves have instructed me not to mention that they have a shop in Manhattan called Tender Buttons because they do not want even the dimmest radon after-image of hucksterism to contaminate the labor of love that is this book. But I see no problem since even a quick glance will tell you that Tender Buttons is not a shop but a button museum that happens to deaccession daily in order to keep going.

Tender Buttons is on the ground floor of a button-size town house. The house is only twelve feet wide, and the shop itself is only eight feet wide. Every day in the little display window out front is to be found an exhibition of rare, unusual, or historic buttons. Inside, packed haunch to paunch, shank to flank, elbow to rib, are people from all over the world indulging in the secret vice of setting themselves apart from that mass of humanity who merely feel they have "too many buttons to button and unbutton," to quote, in its entirety, the suicide note of another Danish prince (not Hamlet).

It seems like such a harmless vice, too, for we live in a remarkably quiet and placid era in the long history of buttons. It is an egalitarian era. Outside as well as inside Tender Buttons, repoussé Venetian gold buttons can now lie alongside two-hole plastic buttons from Osaka—and who is going to arch an eyebrow? Five hundred years ago the wearing of buttons made of gold, silver, precious stones, and crystal inspired such scalding resentment that governments passed sumptuary laws regulating their display. Buttons ran, like Tadzio's, from the neck to the waist and from the elbow to the wrist. You could tell status and wealth at a glance by the materials and workmanship of a person's buttons. The nobs looked down on the poor sods who wore buttons of pewter and cut steel rather than of the real articles, which were silver and crystal.

But I won't go on. In the book that lies before us you will see, far better than I can describe it, a world of social competition and an infinity of aesthetic aspirations . . . in buttons. And perhaps you will even agree with me when I say that a throaty continental voice in the darkness has given us the best revelation to date of what was in the heart of Mann's unforgettable von Aschenbach:

"Look, Darling! Those *buttons!* To *die!*"

Enamel and gold, late 19th century

These exquisite gold-mounted enamel moon buttons have a wit and cool beauty that raise them above the merely cute or anecdotal. The liquid-blue backgrounds embellished with minute foil stars, as well as the delicately balanced compositions, make these fairy-tale buttons models of understatement. (enlarged)

INTRODUCTION

e live with buttons all our lives. Small, seemingly insignificant, plentiful, and of proverbially little value, they are, as Jasper Johns said of his own familiar icons, "things the mind already knows."

But, in fact, buttons are richly varied, often exquisitely crafted, imaginatively designed, and made of valuable materials. In their making they reveal our impulse to enhance even the most familiar and minute details of everyday life, and in their collecting they represent our ever-present desire to find the extraordinary in the commonplace. Not only are we amazed by the labor and craftsmanship applied to such tiny objects, but particularly in an age when bigger is better, we are moved simply by the effort someone has taken to make something so small.

There is scant literature on early button collecting, but records of known collections and buttons in museums abroad indicate that there were collectors of buttons at least as early as the nineteenth century. In western Europe, during the Belle Epoque, one of the pastimes of the rich and fashionable was the pursuit and collection of small antiquities, among which were buttons. Many important collections were formed during this period.

Button collecting as an organized activity had its origins in America in the late 1930s. The Depression encouraged the rise of this hobby since it depended less on money than on ingenuity. Vast amounts of buttons—on strings, in boxes, still attached to old clothing—had always been stored away by inadvertent "collectors," and it was in these bewildering and unorganized assortments that the search began.

The earliest collectors, like gold prospectors, excitedly explored the uncharted terrain, searching and researching. Eager to share their findings and anxious to recruit new collectors, these pioneer enthusiasts formed regional clubs and, in 1938, The National Button Society to exchange information and exhibit new finds. It is the legacy of these industrious devotees—their energy in organizing, classifying, and dating, and their scholarship in publishing articles, bulletins, and books—that has created a system and a vocabulary for talking about and collecting buttons.

After World War II, American collectors extended the range of their search to Europe and discovered the extraordinary and valuable buttons from the eighteenth and nineteenth centuries—miniature paintings, gold and jewels, enamel, porcelain, engraved silver, decorated pearl—that had been saved and collected both as antique objects and for their intrinsic worth. At about the same time, European antique dealers immigrating to America brought with them many fine examples. It was during the mid- to late 1950s that American button collecting changed from its grass-roots origins to a sophisticated international pursuit.

What began as a trifle was becoming a collectible. Up to this period it had been possible to accumulate many different types of buttons at modest prices, and time was spent identifying and classifying them. Now, new collectors entered the market with more knowledge and more savvy, and they wanted to purchase top-quality, deluxe examples. Presently, buttons are being sold at auction, as well as by private individuals, dealers, or estates, and prices are competitive, adding to the difficulty and expense of building a new collection. But since more and greater collections are coming into the market, it is—despite the prices—a propitious time to acquire exceptional buttons.

Our own collecting began in the mid-1960s, after we purchased a huge stock of vintage buttons from the 1930s to the 1950s. We were interested in contemporary art, and buttons, like Andy Warhol's soup cans, seemed the perfect focus: irreverent and commonplace. After all, hadn't we both admired the collages of Joseph Cornell and Kurt Schwitters and the object paintings of Jim Dine and Claes Oldenburg? Here then was *our* object—small, round, and basic—with its inherent sense of humor and touch of absurdity.

In 1964 we opened a shop called "Tender Buttons"—the title borrowed from Gertrude Stein—as our statement and our contribution to the avant-garde. Our whimsical notion of the button as modern art soon gave way, however, to the realities of running an increasingly serious and demanding business.

In an outdated issue of a defunct antiques magazine we saw an ad for the Just Buttons museum in Southington, Connecticut. Without investigating, we leapt into a car and raced to the address, arriving just in time to find a "closed" sign. We banged on the door and met Sally Luscomb, the curator, as well as the editor of the journal *Just Buttons,* and author of the indispensable reference *Encyclopedia of Buttons.* This meeting made us aware that there was a world of collectible buttons and a great deal to learn about them. Overwhelmed by an exhibit of buttons beautiful beyond our imagination, we could never have supposed that in twenty years we would purchase the entire museum collection.

One of the best ways to gauge changing attitudes toward buttons over the years is through the type of attention they have received outside of collecting circles. Early interest in our shop was largely confined to fashion publications like *Vogue* and *Harper's Bazaar.* By the 1970s, however, buttons had become a more recognized collectible, and serious general-interest magazines—*The New Yorker* and *Town & Country,* for example—began to write about them, and about our shop.

But it was in the 1980s that buttons truly cast off their humble persona. In 1982 the Cooper-Hewitt Museum in New York held an exhibition called "Button, Button," acknowledging the new importance of this tiny object, and the Smithsonian Institution in Washington held an exhibition celebrating Halley's comet and included buttons among the objects displayed. By the end of the decade, even financial publications like *Forbes* and *The Wall Street Journal* were paying attention to buttons as expensive items with investment cachet.

While our shop flourished, our own commitment and approach to collecting changed and grew. We traveled everywhere with the single purpose of finding beautiful buttons, and our initial collection of vintage examples expanded to include rarer and more remarkable buttons from the eighteenth century to the twentieth.

The anecdotes and adventures of our years of collecting are as numerous as the buttons we have accumulated. The people we met, the places we went, and the buttons we unearthed have made lives of occupation, dedication, and excitement.

There is always an anticipatory thrill, beginning after the telephone rings or a letter is received, when we hear that there is one button or many available somewhere in the world—and never anywhere ordinary. We have always set out immediately, like two Gullivers, enjoying the preparation and the pursuit.

On one such trip, we were picked up at our hotel in Paris and taken on a delightfully winding road to the charming village of Meudon, where we stopped at a small castle, in which a fantastic collection of eighty huge leather-bound volumes filled the dining room. This most remarkable and historical record of the buttons of Albert Parent et Cie was an invaluable documentation of fine-arts and crafted buttons of the nineteenth century. How did the great-grandson of this French entrepreneur find us? In an article in a French magazine about our shop.

Years before, our very first *coup de bouton* had been related to this find. A New York button manufacturer had called to say he was going out of business and wanted to sell a well-known exhibit of French buttons, discovered in a barn in France. Known as the La Ruche Collection, with a beehive logo, it contained thousands of fine, collectible buttons mounted in ten large, gilded frames, each packed in a custom-made trunk, with brass hardware, covered with labels from around the world.

This collection had been a traveling display, which was shown—and often competed—at European trade shows, fairs, and exhibitions. The buttons were mounted on velvet, in artful arrangements, which included bronze medals of merit from many countries. Most of the buttons were made by Albert Parent et Cie.

During a record heat of August, we raced to see Zula Fricks, a fabled button collector and dealer in New Orleans, who had finally decided to sell her fabulous collection, gathered over years of travel abroad. When we arrived for our meeting, she could not be found. We spent days in a charming French Quarter hotel, sweltering and staring at the ceiling fans. Finally, after a week of puzzlement and disappointment, we bought two tickets to Mexico.

Maracas in hand, we returned to the hotel to find a note that Mrs. Fricks was in a quarantine room of a New Orleans hospital. Dressed in white gowns, mumbling through face masks, we negotiated and purchased one of the finest button collections, the foundation of our own, many pieces from which appear in this book.

Other button escapades have led us to a cave in Brussels, a Quonset hut outside of London, the head of a fjord in Finland, a souk in Cairo, a thrift shop in Moscow, backstage at the Paris Opera, and sometimes to our own backyard: a Manhattan law firm invited us to view buttons from the estate of a client, whose husband, Joseph Stawski, was one of the earliest and foremost European antiques dealers specializing in rare eighteenth- and nineteenth-century buttons. The quality and rarity of his buttons were legendary, and the twenty-block taxi ride to the lawyers' office was as breathless and exciting as any of our trips abroad. We entered a meeting room, a vault was opened, and wrinkled shopping bags full of exquisite buttons were poured onto the huge conference table. These buttons are among the most prized in our collection.

More fantastic than the places buttons have taken us are the people they've introduced to us. Whether a Zen Buddhist divesting himself of earthly possessions or a rabbi in Brooklyn who in mid-negotiation stopped to pray, we have always found ourselves in unique situations, all the more fun and often funny, because after all, it was all about a button.

The buttons in this book were chosen with particular regard for their beauty and artfulness, emphasizing their visual aspects, as well as their significance as collectibles. The overwhelming quantity and variety of buttons makes it impossible to have included every type. We have given a short history of buttonmaking and a description of the techniques and motifs employed, organizing the images and text chronologically by century.

Separated from their context, detached from frock coat or morning dress, antique buttons present numerous difficulties, leaving collectors to solve mysteries of time, place, and construction. Therefore, we have sometimes been forced to give broad dates and to query origins or materials.

Our aim is to reveal to the reader the workmanship and imagination of the buttons presented, to encourage the eye to linger on small, easily overlooked details, and to illustrate how surprisingly captivating a button can be. We want to restore these buttons to the rich historical contexts in which they were produced, worn, admired, and prized.

Today, more than any time since perhaps in the eighteenth century, buttons are objects of importance. As consulting curator Carl C. Dauterman prophetically wrote in a 1940 Cooper-Hewitt exhibition article, "What future is there for buttons? . . . Perhaps they will enjoy a second golden age."

THE EIGHTEENTH CENTURY

Enamel, English, late 18th century

The maker of these exquisite buttons mimicked the art of French porcelain manufacturers of the period by choosing favorite bucolic themes and bordering them with the strong rose-pink color known as "roze." This color was so closely linked to the eighteenth century that it became known in the following century as "Rose Pompadour" or "Rose du Barry," after two well-known mistresses of Louis XV.

Mother-of-pearl, probably French, 18th century

These buttons—most likely intended for men's
court dress—suggest the amount of skill, material,
and labor that went into the creation of a single
button. The mother-of-pearl disks are embellished
with brilliants, steel, cut steel, foil, and gold mesh.

Passementerie, probably French, 18th century

The technique of decorating fabric with metallic threads or paste stones is known as "passementerie," the French term for edgings of gold and silver braid. This assortment of eighteenth-century buttons reveals the special fascination of passementerie, its odd mix of elegance and intimacy, seeming to invoke the living presence of the wearer.

Stone, Ancient Near East

Although the first written record of buttons does not occur until the twelfth century, button-like objects have been discovered in excavations in Egypt, Iran, and Greece. These so-called prehistoric buttons may not have been fasteners in the modern sense of the term: Nevertheless, as this group demonstrates, their construction often suggests that they were attached to fabric of some sort. Their similarity to modern buttons attests to the timelessness of good, utilitarian design.

Buttons belong to the category of things that are always already there. As with any number of such items whose presence is taken for granted, the details of their origins are lost in the amorphous terrain of our prehistory. The first recorded use of the word, "boton," appears in the twelfth-century *Chanson de Roland.* But that appearance—in a disdainful phrase that compares buttons to the counsels of pride—suggests that the objects themselves had been around long enough to acquire popular connotations. In fact, objects constructed much like modern buttons, with openings at the backs and centers and made from gold, glass, bone, stone, and earthenware, have been found in excavations from ancient Persia, Greece, and Egypt. But whether these "prehistoric buttons," some of which date from as early as 2000 B.C., were actually used to fasten clothing remains a question. It seems more likely that they were worn as beads, badges, or ornaments.

Paintings, prints, sculptures, and other representations of clothing provide the most information about how and by whom buttons have been worn. A coin dating from around the eighth century, for instance, shows the Holy Roman Emperor, Lothair, in a flowing mantle gathered and held together around the neck by three buttons. Medieval images and effigies portray the rows of small, close-set buttons that lined the sleeves and bodices of men's and women's clothing into the Renaissance. And endless portraits from the sixteenth and seventeenth centuries picture the dazzling displays of ornamental buttons that embellished the gowns, doublets, and breeches of nobles and aristocrats, or the plain and sober disks worn by clergymen and Dutch merchants.

In addition to visual sources, literary descriptions and inventories from shops and households can tell us the types of buttons that were bought and sold in any period. Moreover, something of the larger social scene in which buttons circulated can be gleaned from legislation aimed at governing their manufacture and use. Etienne Boileau's *Mastery of Trades,* dating from the mid-thirteenth century, for instance, documents the separation of buttonmakers according to the materials they used and thus reveals the rigidly organized and rigorously governed craft system within which buttons were included until the eighteenth century.

Nevertheless, anyone interested in a full account of buttons as cultural and social artifacts will find that specific information is scant. Understandably, individuals rarely felt a need to comment upon these simple everyday objects. But for the historian of buttons, too, the values bestowed upon buttons are inevitably caught up in the web of economic, aesthetic, and social structures of daily life. The narrative history of buttons, then, begins with snatches of descriptions and random comments scattered through accounts that are primarily concerned with other things; where it leads is as vast and varied as history itself.

The eighteenth century is without doubt the golden age of the button. Previously confined to utilitarian or ornamental duties, buttons seem to take on a new mobility throughout the century, moving between art, craft, and increasingly, machine production. Developments in men's clothing at the end of the seventeenth century were the most immediate impetus for the burgeoning production of buttons. Overcoats, or "surtouts," worn through the first quarter of the eighteenth century, were made more close-fitting and were lengthened from the waist to mid-calf, thus calling for even more buttons than before. Typically, an eighteenth-century coat sported buttons at the sleeves, pockets, and along most of the length of the front opening; in addition, at least ten smaller buttons were needed to fasten waistcoats and eight or more for fastening the bottoms of breeches.

Changing styles account for the increase in the number and also the size of buttons but fail to explain the enormous variety of buttons that begins to appear in the eighteenth century. More buttons do not necessarily mean more different kinds; and, in fact, men's coats maintained the fabric and metal buttons of the previous centuries well into the 1700s. One answer to the question of what spawned this multiplicity may be found in the changing structure of fashion itself. Prior to the eighteenth century in Europe, clothing had a fixed meaning: it denoted rank. The right to wear certain styles, materials, and ornaments was determined by social class, itself determined usually by bloodlines. The introduction of the very notion of "fashion" as something unstable, ephemeral, and accessible to anyone who could afford it corresponded to the decline of a class system based on birth. And as the eighteenth century progressed, fashion became an open field in which powerful influences came into play.

The first decades of the century were marked by the Baroque tastes of the previous one. Fabric-covered and embroidered buttons continued to outnumber all other kinds, although here, too, the urge was toward greater variety and excess. The fourteenth-century French embroidering technique called "passementerie" found an enthusiastic audience among the nobility of the eighteenth century, and buttons of silver and gold threads interwoven with sequins, pearls, paste, and other glittering materials complemented the rich fabrics and extraordinary embroidery of men's and women's elaborate dress. So popular were these buttons that imitations were made in more durable metal versions with stamped passementerie patterns.

Precious-metal buttons, in use since the Middle Ages, remained significant indices of wealth and social standing in the early eighteenth century. Hallmarks, too—first introduced to Europe in the thirteenth century to ensure against the sale of inferior silver—persisted as indicators of quality. Especially in England, where hallmark standards were extremely stringent, the type and quality of metals used, and often the maker and company name, were considered signs of distinction. In the mid-eighteenth century silver might still distinguish gentlemen's buttons from those of the working class, which would be of silver plate, white metal, pewter, steel, or brass.

Alongside these traditional symbols of wealth and status, there emerged new ones that more fully captured the spirit of eighteenth-century social mobility. The meteoric rise to popularity of paste jewelry and buttons in the 1730s exemplifies this new social order based not on birthright but on wealth, which was announced by extravagant display. Methods for imitating precious gems had existed since the Egyptians. But the success of Georges Frédéric Strass—an eighteenth-century Parisian jeweler credited with perfecting the technique and organizing the production of these glass jewels into a veritable industry—is without parallel. It seems likely that the initial impulse behind paste was precisely to provide a less costly alternative to diamonds; early paste jewels were colorless, often rose-cut, and usually set in styles that closely followed those of contemporary diamond jewelry. Nevertheless, within a short time the qualities that distinguished paste from diamonds, such as its greater malleability and versatility, came to be recognized as virtues and generated a dazzling array of designs. By mid-century, pastes were made both clear and opalescent and in a wide range of shapes and colors; in France and England especially they were esteemed at least as highly as authentic jewels.

Pastes, gilt, and foil belonged to a world that admired surface over substance. By the second quarter of the eighteenth century, social life was taking place primarily in glittering halls, where mirrors and gaslight transformed the richly colored fabrics and ornaments worn by men and women into fleeting reflections and magically splendid visions. This fascination with surface and appearance found expression in the aesthetics of the Rococo. In the realm of painting, this meant a shift from the rhetorical, edifying images sanctioned by the French Academy in the seventeenth century to images of reverie that addressed the demands and desires of the aristocrats and wealthy bourgeoisie of the eighteenth century. The *fêtes galantes* of Antoine Watteau, a painter whose early training, significantly, included fashion plates and theatrical decorations, established the features of this new mode: an emphasis on sheer materiality over message, of color and brushwork over structure, and a penchant for themes of sensual pleasures and mortal love.

Rococo imagery—depictions of amorous couples and beautiful youths in picturesque landscapes—finds its way onto a large number of eighteenth-century buttons. Carefully rendered miniature scenes were painted in the style of artists such as Watteau and Boucher. In fact, Jean-Honoré Fragonard, the gifted pupil of Boucher and Chardin, is supposed to have painted at least one set of underglass buttons in the manner of Watteau. In addition, the widespread circulation of prints after works by these artists made it possible to replicate exerpts from their paintings, and in many instances one can match images on buttons to their original sources.

Fabric, metal, and jeweled buttons all reflect the notion of the button as ornament. With the advent of representational images on buttons, the tangibility of the surface gave way to a new notion of these objects as portable paintings, akin to the miniatures worn as pendants or pins at around the same period. Not only Rococo scenes, but portraits, historical events, theatrical performances, and touristic views of buildings, monuments, and faraway places were among the many subjects that were set in buttons. The prevailing practice of producing sets of from five to thirty-five made it possible to present whole storylines in sequence across a set, as well as to make sets with different but related designs: assorted millinery styles, commedia dell'arte characters, or mythological motifs, for instance.

The methods for rendering these subjects encompassed most of the techniques known to arts and crafts at the time: enameling, painting, or drawing on paper, ivory, porcelain, and even silk. One technique for decorating with pigment that was especially popular in buttonmaking involved painting on the back side of the front glass (called "reverse painting") and then setting the glass against grounds of different materials. The space left between motif and ground in this reverse painting allowed light to pass through the image and created a sensation of depth, which could be enhanced by painting part of the image on the background.

Two other variants of reverse painting were also commonly found on buttons: silhouettes and églomisé. Silhouettes, painted or made from cut paper, reached the height of their popularity in the eighteenth century; they were named after Etienne de Silhouette, a finance minister to Louis XV, who made them as a pastime. Eglomisé, an ancient technique that was revived in France by a picture-frame maker named Glomy, was an especially rich-looking decoration in which designs etched out of gold paint were subsequently filled in with a layer of black pigment.

By the second half of the eighteenth century differences that had marked the developments of buttonmaking in its two European centers, France and England, crystalized. In France, button production was still organized along the lines of an age-old craft tradition, and the quintessentially French buttons from the eighteenth century are those that involved the artisan's skills: intricate ivory-carved buttons from Dieppe, for example, or the jewel-like enamels from Limoges.

Across the channel, by contrast, the production of buttons was located more and more within the domain of technology and industry. In England, the most famous names associated with buttonmaking are also some of the most important names behind England's emergence as the first industrial leader of the modern world.

Carved ivory, French, late 18th century

The technique for producing these painstaking outline carvings involves gluing thin sheets of ivory to wood and then carving through both with a fine graver. Dieppe, the historic ivory-carving center of France, was renowned for this type of miniature work, and it seems likely that these buttons—which closely resemble eighteenth-century box lids from Dieppe—were produced there as well. Ruby-colored foil and a dark ground show through the lacy ivory to accentuate the skillful carving. The top button has a paste border, the lower is mounted in gilt; both are under glass.

The production of jasperware buttons with cut-steel borders beginning in 1773 marks the joining of two of the most important and best-known of these industrialists, Josiah Wedgwood and the Birmingham steel manufacturer Matthew Boulton. Wedgwood's zealous drive to innovate distinguished his efforts from those of the great ceramic manufacturers who preceded him. By the 1770s Wedgwood's jasperware buttons were available in five colors and a variety of shapes, with many bearing the Neoclassical motifs that became the Wedgwood signature. In addition, Wedgwood not only sold his jasperware medallions for button decoration, he himself also sold finished buttons, with shanks attached.

Boulton, too, stands as a maverick among innovators. Cut-steel buttons were one of the most popular types in the last three decades of the eighteenth century. Originally produced as diamond substitutes, their polished, faceted surfaces, although highly susceptible to rust, created dazzling effects and were, in the words of a contemporary journal, "the leading fashion of the day." By the last quarter of the century there were, therefore, many manufacturers of steel buttons in Birmingham. But Boulton's brilliance in business (it was he who approached Wedgwood to suggest their collaboration) and talent for good management and

Jasperware and cut steel, English, late 18th century

These jasperware buttons, made by Josiah Wedgwood, not only reflect artistic tastes of the eighteenth century, they also record innovations in mass production. By the mid-1770s Wedgwood had perfected his pottery production techniques to the point where he could offer five basic color grounds for his cameo designs, including the characteristic blue pictured here. The cut-steel settings were the creation of Matthew Boulton, a steel manufacturer who collaborated with Wedgwood in the 1770s. The facets are meant to imitate precious stones.

This group of buttons, with rolled enamel rims, is reminiscent of those made by Battersea, the famous London enamel factory; they may, however, have been produced in Bilston, South Staffordshire. The first Bilston factory was opened in 1749, and production continued until 1831. Like Battersea, Bilston was famous for small enameled objects, such as snuffboxes, scent bottles, etuis, and bonbonnières, many of which bore floral motifs similar to these.

organization have made him by far the best known; indeed, collectors often, and misleadingly, use the term "Boulton steels" to describe all faceted-steel buttons similar to those made by his firm.

Transfer printing is another buttonmaking innovation that originated within the English small-wares industry, probably around mid-century. The technique, which involves transferring designs from copperplates to ceramics, was probably developed at the Battersea enamel factory and quickly replaced painting on all but the finest ceramic goods. Finally, at the end of the century, when the buttons made from mother-of-pearl began to rival in popularity those of steel, Birmingham again became a primary center of manufacture.

Industry and history, too, had a decisive impact on the development of decorative arts in the second half of the eighteenth century. The archaeological discoveries at Herculaneum and Pompeii made the classical past into a repository of motifs and forms for artists and designers. Beginning in the 1760s, the nostalgic longing for the ideals and values of the ancients made Neoclassicism a major style in every art form.

However, far from simply inspiring slavish imitations of Greek and Roman artifacts, the new reverence for classical antiquity engendered a wide range of responses. If Wedgwood's coolly elegant reliefs, drawn, as they seem to be, from

Greek vases, exemplify one aspect of Neoclassicism as it emerged in the decorative arts, then the rash of cherubic cupids that adorn objects throughout the period exemplify another. These boisterous children, offspring of the Roman god of love, reflect the merging of the Rococo and Neoclassical that occurred in the late eighteenth century.

Buttons documented the rediscovery of the past; they also documented the birth of the future. In the aftermath of the French Revolution, Revolutionary motifs appeared on buttons of every conceivable kind. A large number of these bore symbols and slogans declaring allegiance to the cause, while others either chronicled the events or commemorated the personalities of the Revolution.

By comparison, there are few representational buttons depicting the American Revolution thirteen years earlier. One rare example, in the present collection, is an extraordinary set of diamond-trimmed buttons, made in France, depicting the participation of French troops in the War of American Independence. Still, independence did make its mark on the American button industry. Prior to the Revolution, British trade restrictions ensured that buttons worn in the colonies, especially the most sumptuous and extravagant ones, were imported from England. Metal buttons were one important exception. Throughout the century

French, late 18th century

These radiant diamond-trimmed and gold-mounted buttons depict the participation of French troops in the American Revolution with a combination of reportage and melodrama typical of eighteenth-century history painting. In 1778 France joined the American colonies in their battle against the British. In 1783 the Parisian engravers F. Godefroy and N. Ponce published a book of sixteen prints depicting events during the War of American Independence, three of which appear here: the taking of the island of Grenada, the surprise attack on St. Eustatius, and the Battle of Saratoga. The scenes on the two buttons at bottom have yet to be identified.

Drawing on silk, probably French, 18th century

This button is an imaginative combination of Neo-classical sobriety and Rococo suggestiveness. Although the symbolic significance, if any, is unclear, the image itself is self-explanatory: A woman partially draped in Neoclassical robes demonstrates a geometric proof. The design is drawn or printed on white silk and mounted under glass with a copper rim. (enlarged) buttons of silver, pewter, copper, and brass were made by silversmiths, jewelers, coin makers, and other artisans whose primary trade was in other goods. Silver buttons were, in fact, among the many silver items used for barter with the Indians. It was not until after the Revolution, however, that, freed from manufacturing restrictions, buttonmaking emerged as an industry in and of itself. It seems appropriate, therefore, that the most valued of all American buttons are the stamped metal ones made for the inauguration of George Washington in 1789.

One other development in buttons, specific to and typical of the late eighteenth century, is the introduction of minutely observed animals and especially insects as decorative motifs. Complete sets of elegant buttons, in hand-painted glass or gemstone and quartz, depicting insects of all sorts, recall the specimen books and natural-history engravings of the period. The scientific study of animals progressed steadily throughout the century, aided by improvements in the microscope and abetted by the spirit of empiricism that led scientists and amateurs alike to investigate the entire natural world. The publication of the comte de Buffon's

(opposite)
Reverse painting, French,
late 18th century

The events and figures of the French Revolution were documented on a vast range of buttons. These reverse-painted buttons, mounted in copper, belong to a larger set relating the march to Versailles and the encampment in narrative sequence. Words to the popular song "A Ça ira" ("All Will Be Well") are inscribed in the blank space at the bottom of each scene.

Reverse painting, French, mid to late 18th century

Realistically rendered insects have been a recurrent theme in the decorative arts. These buttons, reverse painted and backed with a thin leaf of white wax, prove how elegant their depiction can be; in fact, the comte de Buffon, the great eighteenth-century naturalist, is purported to have painted insect buttons of extreme realism and delicacy. Gold, blue, and black borders similar to these but in slightly different patterns occur on other insect buttons and may be the mark of a particular artist. All are under glass and mounted in brass borders.

monumental *Histoire naturelle* beginning in 1749 marked a new emphasis on observation over imagination and served as source and inspiration for countless buttons, including the "habitat" buttons made from dried animal and plant specimens. In the Age of Enlightenment the potential for the accumulation and ordering of knowledge seemed limitless, and buttons recorded that optimism. Indeed, in his great *Encyclopedia*, the eighteenth-century *philosophe* Denis Diderot devotes eight pages to the subjects of buttons, buttonmakers, and even buttonholes, including illustrations of button styles, materials, tools, and methods of construction.

(below)
Reverse painting, late 18th century

The shattering social and political up-
heavals of the late eighteenth century produced an unprecedented sense of a break
with, and nostalgia for, the past. The
themes and objects in this group of buttons are typical of the period: utopian
visions of a preindustrial, untroubled existence. Left and right are miniature tab-
leaux, reminiscent of the picturesque
landscapes of Gainsborough or Valen-
ciennes. The motifs at top and bottom
resemble elements popular in contemporary printed textiles and wallpapers. The
vase, especially, is typical of the attenu-
ated, decorative forms of Neoclassicism
inspired by the archaeological discoveries
at Pompeii and Herculaneum earlier
in the century.

(opposite)
Reverse painting, 18th century

These buttons are an intriguing synthesis of the elegant and the naive, depicting long-nosed animals reverse painted on glass, with lustrous mica backgrounds, in copper mountings. According to the legend that accompanied it, this set belonged to a lady-in-waiting to Catherine the Great.

(right)
Découpage, probably French, 18th century

These gilt-rimmed rustic scenes were made by layering pieces of cut paper in a process called "découpage." Here, the landscape details were probably painted on specially treated paper, while the architectural structures were cut out and appliquéd to give a sense of texture and depth. (enlarged)

(opposite right)
Reverse painting, probably French, 18th century

The combination of silhouettes and sepia tones gives these scenes the three-dimensional look of paper cutouts. In addition, the background is painted in watercolor on paper, while the rest is painted in oil on the reverse of the glass; they are set in decorative gilt borders. The juxtaposition of classical and rustic elements seems odd now but is not at all unusual for the eighteenth century.

Painting on ivory, probably French, 18th century

In both of these buttons the emphasis seems to be on the gentlemen's couture, especially the conspicuously placed hats. The type of hat shown here, made of flexible felt or beaver with flat or upturned brim, was primarily a rural style but was also widely adopted by the elderly and the conservative in city and country.

Engraving on paper, late 18th century

The makeshift construction of these buttons suggests that they were not intended for the haute bourgeoisie. The hand-colored prints set in brass rims under glass, which depict such gentlemanly activities as drinking, playing instruments, and tipping the hat, reveal something of the tremendous ceremony that governed even the most mundane activities in the eighteenth century.

Watercolor on paper, French, late 18th or early 19th century

These fashionable figures from the late eighteenth or early nineteenth century are printed on paper and colored quite lavishly by hand.

Reverse painting, French, 18th century

The silhouette took its name from Etienne de Silhouette, a finance minister to Louis XV who practiced the technique as a pastime. Silhouette images, whether painted or made from cut paper, were especially popular in the eighteenth century. Although they could be quite complex, these somewhat crude-looking copper-mounted, reverse-painted buttons reveal another aspect of their appeal: the absence of color and detail made them extremely simple for amateurs to produce.

Various materials, 18th century

Shown here are four buttons made of various materials typical of the eighteenth century: (from left to right) a "habitat" button made with shells and dried foliage under glass; a button of slag glass; a painted bouquet on porcelain with a steel inner border and a copper rim; and a rare rebus button, painted on ivory, bearing the double motto "She has conquered my heart" and "I loved without diversion."

Painting on ivory, French, 18th century

These histrionic figures in Neoclassical costume differ from most eighteenth-century depictions of actors in that they seem to be neither stock characters nor portraits of famous actors in character. However, these finely painted buttons, in copper rims, mounted under glass, reflect the eighteenth-century fascination with theater in particular and with artifice and appearances in general.

Semiprecious stone, 18th century

The variegated form of chalcedony known as "agate" is an ideal decorative stone because of its patterning and naturally rich tones. This group of buttons reveals the variety and natural opulence of agate; only the metal frames and pin shanks provide any additional ornament for the thinly cut and highly polished stones.

Mother-of-pearl, French, 18th century

In these richly embellished buttons
mother-of-pearl is used as a luminous
ground for striking patterns of
enamel and paste brilliants.

Mosaic, Italian, late 18th century

These buttons, set in simple brass mountings, are rare late-eighteenth-century glass micromosaics. The demand for depictions of ruins and replicas of antique wall paintings resulted from the archaeological discoveries of the eighteenth century and the increase in tourism to Florence and Rome. The Roman Giacomo Raffaelli is credited with the invention of micromosaics—mosaics made out of tiny fragments of colored glass, or "tesserae"—in the 1770s.

(opposite)
Enamel and gold, 18th century

This large button is remarkable for the quality and extent of detail throughout. The hand-painted scene, in its bustling activity and complicated perspective, recalls city views painted for tourists at the time by such artists as Canaletto. The border is elaborately hand-tooled in gold; the back is also gold. (enlarged)

(right)
Painting on ivory, probably French,
18th century

These buttons picturing frolicking cherubs are part of a larger set of buttons painted on ivory, under glass, and set in gilded-copper mountings. According to theological doctrine, cherubim were members of the second order of angels, but by the eighteenth century they more typically appeared as rambunctious children, often displaying naughty or lascivious behavior.

(left)
Sulphide, probably French, late
18th century

The type of glasswork known as "sulphide" actually entails enclosing porcelaneous white material in clear crystal glass. Although apparently invented in France, the method was introduced into England and patented there by Apsley Pellatt in the early nineteenth century. These buttons are set against textured backgrounds in gilded copper borders.

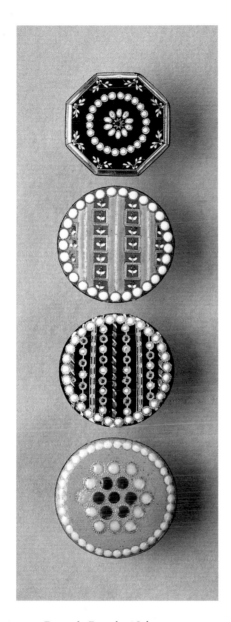

Enamel, French, 18th century

These fantastically decorated buttons would have been especially startling against the rich floral brocades of a man's court dress. The Rococo artisan left no surface unadorned, embellishing the smallest objects with a multitude of patterns.

Mother-of-pearl, French, 18th century

These buttons are brilliant examples of ajouré, a technique in which pearl is pierced or carved to produce intricate openwork patterns. Here, the designs are further enhanced with pastes, foil, and large central "jewels" of enamel (top) and paste. (enlarged)

Reverse painting, French, 2nd half of 18th century

Attitudes toward children changed markedly from the mid-eighteenth century on as childhood began to be perceived as distinct from adulthood in psychological, social, and biological terms. With this new perception of children came an increased attention to their behavior and upbringing. Mounted in copper rims, under glass, these rare French buttons, addressed "to good children," seem to be didactic, offering instruction in duties and pleasures; the hint of menace is probably simply an effect of the naive drawing, which produces skewed proportions and odd expressions.

Painting on ivory, French, 18th century

These painted-ivory buttons with ivory backs, in copper rims, recall popular fashion plates of the period. The settings and postures seem intended to highlight the accoutrements of the fashionable men and women pictured in pastoral pursuits.

Watercolor and pastel painting, English, late 18th century

The centrality of children in late-eighteenth-century art is partially rooted in a yearning, typical of Romanticism, for primitive states of being. These English pastel and watercolor buttons, brass rimmed and under glass, suggest the link between childhood and nature through both subject and style. The landscapes, children, and dog are rendered in soft and similar tones that unify the elements of the scenes.

(above)
Various materials, French, late 18th to early 19th century

These meltingly beautiful depictions of romantically absorbed couples perfectly express the premises of French Rococo painting; the soft focus and languid postures enhance the sense of reverie and inspire the viewer's fantasy. The center button is hand-painted porcelain, while the buttons to the left and right are paintings on ivory under glass. All are mounted in brass.

Painting on ivory, probably French, 18th century

This group of painted-ivory buttons, set in decorated copper borders, present three pervasive eighteenth-century female types. The mythologically inspired figures at top and bottom may be specific representations of Erato, the muse of lyric poetry, and Athena, the goddess of wisdom. The shepherdess is another favorite literary and decorative motif.

Mother-of-pearl, French, mid-18th century

These carved mother-of-pearl buttons are part of a larger set of twelve or possibly more, each of which relates one scene of an elaborate love story. The last button finds the blissful lovers in a typical Rococo scene. In the eighteenth century, large sets—from five to thirty-five—were often worn sequentially down a man's frock coat.

Mother-of-pearl, French, 18th century

These carved-pearl rebus buttons reveal the eighteenth-century penchant for co-ded communication and intricate court-ship behavior. Pictures, words, and letters are combined to produce mottos, mostly amorous, like the one at center, which, when said aloud, announces "Elle a cédé," or "She has given in."

Painting on ivory, probably French,
18th century

These pastel-colored painted-ivory buttons, under
glass with brass rims, perfectly capture the Rococo
love for the nondramatic moment. The legend
inscribed in stone behind the woman at center
seems to articulate this celebration of languor and
constancy: "toujours la même," that is,
"always the same."

Copper, English or French, late 18th century

These exceptional copper buttons are decorated
with enamel and pin-shanked opaline glass medallions. The borders are chased and gilded.

Painting on ivory, French, mid-18th century

These beautifully detailed and ornamented buttons reflect the French fascination with the East that began early in the eighteenth century. The vogue for "turquerie" in interior design and theatrical productions gained special impetus in 1721 with the visit of a Turkish embassy from the court of the Grand Sultan.

Painting on ivory and paper
English and French, late 18th century

By the end of the eighteenth century, landscape
had emerged as an important category of painting.
These buttons reflect this growing appreciation
for the evocative beauty of nature; the inclusion of
solitary figures, especially, recalls a recurring
motif of Romantic landscape painting. The two
middle buttons are painted on ivory; those at either
end are painted on paper. All are mounted
under glass with copper or brass rims.

Painting on ivory, probably French, 18th century

The baroque compositions of these extraordinary painted-ivory battle scenes recall the great cycles of Rubens. A confused jumble of figures and red, heated tones present a vision of war that is at once violent and heroic, as exemplified in the astonishingly expressive portrayal of a soldier's death on the middle top button.

Painting on paper, French, late 18th century

The system of training horses, known as "dressage," was practiced in ancient Greece. But the term itself has its origin in the eighteenth century, a period that admired precision of movement in humans and animals alike. This boxed set of buttons in silver rims illustrates dressage positions in a series of exquisitely detailed miniature gouache paintings. The paintings and the box itself suggest a late-eighteenth-century date, which cannot, however, be confirmed by the unusual and unidentifiable back mark.

Enamel and silver, late 18th century

In the late eighteenth century, the revived interest in classical style pervaded almost every aspect of culture and imposed a unified look for everything from buildings to buttons. These finely rendered enameled buttons, in silver mountings, depict six of the nine muses; they may have been part of a larger set illustrating all nine.

Enamel and porcelain, late 18th century

This group of assorted enamel and painted-porcelain buttons embraces some of the most typical decorative themes of the eighteenth century: cupids, young lovers, classical figures, and maritime subjects.

*Painting on paper, French,
late 18th century*

Rococo paintings were a common source of images for buttons in both the eighteenth and nineteenth centuries. Prints of works by artists such as Watteau, Boucher, and Lancret were widely disseminated, and it is common to find buttons with the original motifs reversed, indicating that they were taken directly from these reproductions. Although no specific sources have been identified for the buttons pictured here, the erotic allusiveness, the virtuoso painting, as well as the gemlike paste borders, are clearly meant to recall the luxurious pleasures of the Rococo.

(opposite)
*Paste, French and English, late 18th to
early 19th century*

The eighteenth century saw an enormous increase in the popularity of paste jewelry and buttons as result both of changes in social life and advances in technique. These buttons reveal the qualities of paste that contributed to its appeal. Unlike conventional gemstones, pastes could be cut to any shape and produced in a wide range of colors. In addition, because the stones were light, the metal settings, often silver, could be thin and unobtrusive. The milky, or opaline, pastes pictured here were made in the period between 1780 and 1820 in England and France; both countries excelled in the production of pastes.

*Silver, Austro-Hungarian,
probably 17th century*

This group of ornate cast, pierced, and gilded silver buttons, with enamel, jeweled, and filigree decoration, probably dates from the seventeenth century and is said to be of Austro-Hungarian origin. Decorative patterns almost identical to some of these appear on wall sconces at Schönbrunn, the palace of Maria Theresa in Vienna. The large floral button at center is a rarity, known as a "smuggler's button": The top unscrews to reveal a small compartment for holding secret messages and small contraband, such as precious jewels or opium.

(opposite)
Porcelain, French, 18th century

These colorful painted-porcelain buttons illustrate specific birds with botanical detail in the manner of naturalist prints of the period.

Porcelain, Denmark, late 18th century

These painted-porcelain buttons bear the back mark of the Royal Copenhagen factory, one of the largest producers of hard-paste buttons at the time. The stripes and stylized floral patterns reflect contemporary fashions, as do the striking color combinations.

Porcelain, Denmark, late 18th century

These glazed white-porcelain buttons were produced by Royal Copenhagen in the late eighteenth century. The center button is turned to show the typical back mark of three wavy blue lines. The buttons at left and right reveal simple and elegant pierced decorations.

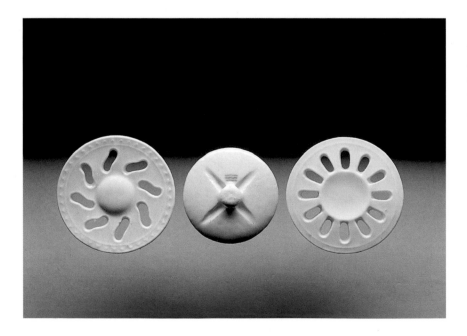

*Silver, various countries,
late 17th century*

The shanks and shapes of these bauble-like silver buttons suggest that they may have originally been attached to thin bars by means of a link. "Link," or "toggle," buttons, as they are known, have been made since the sixteenth century and are probably of Dutch or German origin. Although once a standard fastener for men's coats and breeches, they are now extremely scarce. The silver link buttons that survive today are almost impossible to date.

Copper and brass, probably American, 1789

Worn in honor of the 1789 inauguration of George Washington, these buttons served the same purpose as more recent political paraphernalia and are among the most sought-after American historical buttons. This group shows four of twenty-three different patterns recognized as genuine in both coat (large) and breech (small) sizes. All depict various combinations of slogans, patriotic symbols, and Washington's initials; the "GW" with a "linked-states" border at left is notable for its close resemblance to the 1776 Continental dollar. "Washington Inaugurals," as these buttons are called, were produced in copper, brass, and silver plate and are usually flat with brazed-on shanks. Although their precise origins are not clear, they were probably made in the colonies by coin makers and other metalworkers.

Copper, French, late 18th century

These gilt-copper buttons engraved with patriotic slogans and emblems date from the decade after the French Revolution. The "bonnet rouge," or "liberty cap," shown in several variations, became an important symbol of Revolutionary ideology after 1792, when Louis XVI donned the cap as an attempt at pacification and a gesture of good will.

Copper, probably English, 18th century

Some of the most attractive and well-made commercial copper buttons were manufactured in the last three decades of the eighteenth century. Most of them were produced in England and exported to France. The buttons pictured are more unusual than the conventionally patterned coppers: The three large buttons feature engraved and chased pastoral scenes; the one at far left bears the Masonic emblem.

Copper, probably English, 18th century

Although the term "colonial coppers" is often used by collectors as a general designation for eighteenth-century copper buttons, it is rightfully applied only to buttons from the American colonies. This group includes a wide range of coppers, both typical and rare; the oval, pierced, and scalloped buttons are especially unusual.

Silver, English, late 18th century

These engraved silver buttons celebrate the advent of ballooning in the eighteenth century. The first successful balloon ascent was made on June 4, 1783, by the Montgolfier brothers, who are pictured in two buttons at top. Shortly afterward, Paris boutiques marketed buttons "à la Montgolfière" and "au ballon." The group shown here depicts the images and dates of successful maiden voyages.

Silver, English, 1810

This presentation set of engraved silver buttons and buckles was produced in 1810 to commemorate the fiftieth year of the colorful reign of George III. The British king and queen, who were typically depicted as models of sober domesticity, are surrounded here by some of the major political, military, and artistic figures of the period, including Edmund Burke, Horace Walpole, Adam Smith, and William Blake.

Silver, English, 18th century

The striking feature of the group above is the dog's name at the top of each of these engraved silver buttons made by Samuel Davenport of London. The vogue for sentimental depictions of dogs reached a peak in the nineteenth century, but these buttons, probably from the late eighteenth century, belong instead to the tradition of English sporting scenes. The "good country life" provides the context for the hallmarked silver buttons at right. Engraved buttons such as these reveal the way in which the accoutrements associated with rural activities, like riding and hunting, shaped the appearance of men's fashion in general.

Silver, American, 1st half of 18th century

The back mark on these silver buttons, a "PG" inside a rectangle, identifies them as the work of the American silversmith Philip Goulet, and locates them most likely in the first half of the eighteenth century. The wonderful engraved depictions of wild animals recall prints in bestiaries and natural-history manuals of the period and seem to be a combination of empirical observation and preconceived notions.

Enamel, French, late 18th century

The fine workmanship of these buttons is evident
in the animation and movement of the playful
scenes. The intricately cut-out gold-foil figures,
foliage, and animals are placed on a striking cobalt-
blue guilloché enamel ground; the backs
are counter-enameled. (enlarged)

Enamel and gilt, French, 18th century

The luster of these exquisite buttons is the result of the guilloché enameling: The background is engraved with patterns of lines and then covered with transparent cobalt-blue enamel, which allows light to reflect off the metal surface in shimmering waves. The painted gold figures and the chased, gilded mountings give these buttons an additional air of elegance.

Overleaf:
Portrait miniatures, French, ca. 1790

These fine late-eighteenth-century buttons are painted with portraits of famous personalities from the beginning of the French Revolution, among them M. Barère de Vieuzac (1755–1841), who, as publisher of the newspaper *Point du Jour,* printed the Rights of Man and Citizen; the Vicomte de Mirabeau (1754–1792), who served in the American War of Independence; Mme Louise-Elisabeth Vigée-Lebrun (1755–1842), court painter to Queen Marie Antoinette; and M. Antoine-Pierre-Joseph-Marie Barnave (1761–1793), a lawyer who escorted the royal family to Paris and was later arrested and executed. The names of all the sitters are engraved on the backs of the buttons—a rare feature (and they are reprinted here, with brief identifications, below the photographs on the following pages). Each button is set in silver, with a paste diamond border.

MLLE DESBROSSES
An actress

M. BARÈRE DE VIEUZAC
A lawyer

MLLE OLIVIER
An actress

ANDRÉ-BONIFACE RIQUETTI
Vicomte de Mirabeau

MLLE ROSE DUCREAUX
An artist

M. JEAN-PAUL RABAUT DE
ST. ETIENNE
A deputy of the Third Estate

MME LOUISE-ELISABETH
VIGÉE-LEBRUN
Court painter to Marie
Antoinette

MME DAVID
Possibly the wife of the
painter Jacques-Louis David

MLLE DE LA TOUR
Unidentified

MLLE AMELIE-JULIE
CANDEILLE

An opera singer

AMBROISE POLYCARPE

Duc de la Rochefoucauld

ANNE ANTOINETTE CLAVEL

An opera singer (known as
Mme de Saint-Huberty)

MLLE MARTIN

An actress

MLLE DE VALMON

An actress

"JEUNE DAME ESPAGNOLE"

M. GÉRARD

A fictitious farmer

ALEXANDER THÉODORE
VICTOR

Comte de Lameth

M. ANTOINE-PIERRE-JOSEPH-
MARIE BARNAVE

A lawyer

Various materials, probably Irish and French, 18th and 19th centuries

These buttons, made about a century apart, chart the transformation of a motif. At top, semiprecious stones set on rock crystal and mounted in silver create an insect that conforms to the eighteenth-century demand for realism. The button, said to be Irish, is part of a large set depicting a variety of insects in catalogue manner. At bottom, a fanciful Art Nouveau dragonfly in nonnaturalistic enameled colors with cut-steel trim reveals a more remote relationship to the natural world.

The egalitarian spirit and moral tenor of the nineteenth century stand in sharp relief against the apparent frivolity of the eighteenth. In 1777 a French cartoonist gleefully pictured the rays of light emanating from the cut-steel buttons on a gentleman's jacket and literally bedazzling a lady with their brilliance. In 1836, trembling with puritanical fervor, Thomas Carlyle in his *Sartor Resartus* wrote condemningly of the "Clothes-Wearing Man," whose only aim was to be "a visual object or thing that will reflect rays of light. Your silver or your gold he solicits not; simply the glance of your eyes."

In the realm of buttonmaking, post-Revolutionary moderation marked the end of one era and the beginning of another. As artisans and dealers of luxury items closed shop at the end of the eighteenth century, in the nineteenth century, buttonmaking developed in two distinct but related directions.

On the one hand, it reflected the continuing progress of industrialization. New processes expanded the range of materials from which buttons could be made, and the new technologies of mass production entailed a vast reorganization of the button industry itself. On the other hand, artisan production survived, nourished by encounters with the crafts of other cultures as well as by rediscoveries of traditional techniques. Revivalist tendencies in buttonmaking — in terms of both motifs and techniques — bespoke a nostalgia for what, after the revolutions of the eighteenth century and in the face of industrialization, must have seemed to be a distant and irretrievable past.

Some eighteenth-century motifs that remained popular in the early to mid-nineteenth century conformed, not surprisingly, to the idyllic, fanciful visions that marked the products of Romanticism. Playful cherubs and cupids, lovers, shepherds and shepherdesses, and picturesque landscapes continued to decorate buttons, often surrounded by elaborate borders reminiscent of the gilded wood frames of the previous century. Eighteenth-century fashions were pictured on buttons that were meant to be worn on nineteenth-century dress; for example, the post-Revolutionary fashion extremists known as "incroyables" and "merveilleuses" were evidently considered a fashionable button motif long after their flamboyant costumes and mannerisms were out of fashion.

As new, less time-consuming methods replaced the artisan production of the eighteenth century, the hierarchy of materials shifted. Although only a few fabric buttons are included in most collections of fine buttons, in the nineteenth-century they were, in fact, more generally available than ever before. The invention of the Jacquard loom in 1801 made possible the production of tapestry-like fabrics to rival the handmade passementerie of the seventeenth and eighteenth centuries. Fine fabrics were available not only at lower cost, but also in greater variety. Crochet, silks, damasks, brocades were all used for buttons, and by the end of the century dressmakers, equipped with small, hand-operated buttonmaking ma-

Enamel, French, ca. 1875

The seascapes and harbor scenes on these finely painted enamel buttons are standard motifs of the period. However, the bottom button is highly unusual for its elliptic shape, which is particularly appropriate for the horizontal landscape.

chines, could create their own custom-made fabric buttons to match their client's clothing.

Improvements in construction were another crucial factor in mass production of fabric buttons, and these, too, came in the first quarter of the century. In 1825, Benjamin Sanders, Jr., a Birmingham manufacturer, improved upon his father's remarkable innovation, the cloth-covered button with a metal shank, by inventing the flexible shank; instead of wire, a piece of canvas, through which a needle could pass in any direction, protruded from the back of the button. By the 1830s these buttons were being mass-produced in factories in Britain and the United States.

A later innovation in the mass production of fabric buttons allowed repeated patterns of fairly detailed pictures to be woven into ribbons of fabric on the Jacquard loom. The woven images, known as "textilographs" or "Stevensgraphs," after Thomas Stevens, the Englishman who invented them in the 1860s, resulted from the effort to revive what had been a flourishing ribbon trade in Coventry. The ribbons were supplied to various industries and made into a range of novelty items, including badges, bookmarks, and pictures, by firms in England and France; few buttons of this type appear to have been made, however.

Despite competition from fabric, metal remained a staple ingredient in button-making, in part because it lent itself so readily to mass production. In America, pewter, which had been imported from Britain during the colonial period, continued to supply the button needs of the populace in the early nineteenth century. The low melting point of pewter meant that old housewares could be recast and recycled into buttons by just about anyone with access to a button mold. When British imports were cut off after the Revolution, the task of producing pewter buttons was taken up by the newly empowered American manufacturers. In 1790 the Grilley brothers of Waterbury, Connecticut, founded the first American factory devoted entirely to pewter buttonmaking, although, like many early pewterers, they switched to the manufacture of gilt buttons in the first decades of the new century.

Finely crafted silver and gilt-brass buttons epitomize the sobering turn that aristocratic style took in the early nineteenth century—what Lord Byron called "a certain exquisite propriety," as opposed to the ostentatiousness that preceded it. In the late eighteenth century, the large size of buttons reflected the excesses of men's dress in general; contemporary caricatures of English dandies, for instance, picture them with platter-sized buttons on their coats. By contrast, the course of the early 1800s was personified by Beau Brummel, an arbiter of elegance and intimate of the Prince Regent, who is said to have initiated the trend toward dark, simply cut clothes for men. Buttons for these styles were simpler and smaller, with diameters measuring less than one inch, or about half what they had been. Ever in

Gold, French, early 19th century

The perpetual attraction of gold stems from both its intrinsic brilliance and the associations of wealth and power that have naturally attached to it. These buttons capitalize on both aspects of gold's appeal. The center button, with its opulent patterning and varied tones and textures, is a virtuoso display of the possibilities of the material. The Roman heads set in mother-of-pearl borders allude to the splendor of empire.

the forefront of metal-button production, Birmingham stopped making large gilt-copper buttons in the 1790s, replacing them with smaller ones of gilt brass; by about 1810 these new gilt-brass buttons almost completely replaced all other types on men's coats.

Although the collector's designation "golden-age buttons" (called simply "gilt") has been reserved for the gold-washed brass buttons made between 1830 and 1850, the output of gilt buttons throughout the first half of the nineteenth century deserves to be considered as the zenith of fine metal buttons. The metal-button industry of this period seems to have achieved a fortunate and successful balance between mass production and hand-finishing; brass disks were produced in quantity, then burnished, chased, engraved, or die stamped by hand. From 1800 to 1830, burnishing was the primary mark of distinction among brass buttons. Birmingham manufacturers perfected a method of hand-polishing the gilded metal against a fine-grained stone, which produced a richly glowing surface that was both highly desirable and difficult to emulate, as their American competitors discovered. Beginning in the 1830s, modest designs began to appear; fruit and floral motifs, textures, and conventional patterns were engraved, die stamped, or chased, a technique that required numerous blows to be struck against the surface of the button with a chasing punch. Carved-pearl centers with brass rims, an elegant variation of the golden-age gilt buttons, were also made in Europe and America.

Sporting buttons comprise a special category of fine metal buttons from the first half of the nineteenth century, while other materials, such as pearl, ivory, enamel, and horn, were used less frequently. England was still the primary manufacturer, although France and America also produced fine sporting buttons to meet domestic demands. The rise in popularity of such rural sports as hunting was related to the growth of cities and the disappearance of the countryside, and the often elaborate and beautifully worked motifs decorating sporting buttons

Enamel, probably French, ca. 1880

Orange monochrome designs on white enamel ground makes these buttons both unique and unusually handsome. This set features the pursuits of aristocratic gentlemen: horse-racing, hunting, sailing, and womanizing.

Ivory, American, ca. 1895

"Scrimshaw," a term of American origin, describes any kind of handicraft done aboard a ship, in a wide range of materials. Most often, however, it refers to the type of blackened engraving on whale's teeth or bone ivory pictured here. These rare scrimshaw buttons with rolled rims are said to have been carved by a Maine sea captain in the 1890s and probably depict actual ships.

were meant to evoke these increasingly rare pleasures of the country life. Depictions of game animals and hounds have less in common with the natural-history buttons of the eighteenth century than with buttons showing leisure activities of the late nineteenth. Nor were sporting buttons worn only in the country during sporting events; hunting enthusiasts might well wear them on other occasions, and some exquisite and fragile sporting buttons were no doubt intended for the less strenuous pleasures of the city.

Of the many firms, both English and French, that dominated the history of buttonmaking from the middle of the nineteenth century on, two French firms—Jean-Félix Bapterosse and Albert Parent et Cie—are notable for significant contributions to the utilitarian and luxury button markets.

The humble appearance of the china button belies the significance of the technological development that gave rise to its existence. Prior to the invention in the 1840s of a machine process for the manufacture of porcelain buttons, china clay had to be molded into the appropriate shapes by hand, making their mass production unfeasible. The Bapterosse firm was not the first to mass-produce porcelain buttons; the process was the invention of an Englishman, and the English pottery Minton was probably the first to employ it. With the help of French government funds, however, Bapterosse rapidly took over the lead in the production of utilitarian china buttons. Rumors in Britain at the time maintained that Bapterosse had covertly learned the formula for porcelain while working at an English factory. The gossip may or may not be true; Bapterosse's formula is distinguished from the British one in its use of wet, as opposed to dry, china clay. In any event, Bapterosse's terrific success must be attributed to his business cunning and his understanding, unusual for the date, of the importance of publicity. It was not enough to produce large quantities at low cost; sample cards, stock cards, and labels, printed with the initials "F.B." and often accompanied by a slogan or emblem proclaiming high quality, kept the Bapterosse name in the eyes and minds of the buying public. Over the course of the century the company

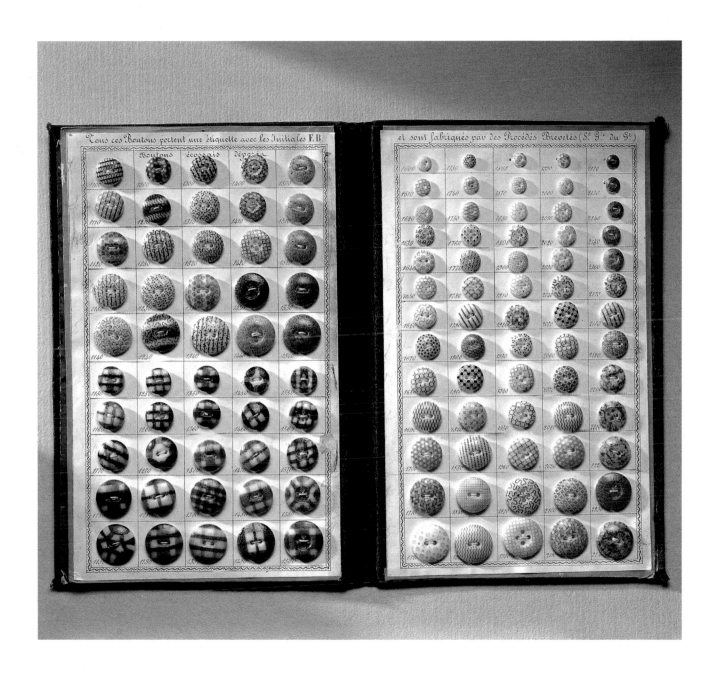

produced a range of porcelain buttons, including those with ivory and pearl-like finishes. But by far the most popular ones among collectors are those with transfer-printed calico patterns (called simply "calicoes") made to match the calico fabrics that were popular from the 1850s.

The success of Albert Parent et Cie, founded in 1825, reflects a broader shift in power in the button industry. The early advent of industrialization in England had given that county an edge in the first half of the century. In order to recapture the button market, the French had, in part, to compete with British industry by introducing the machinery of mass production into their methods. But the brilliance of French manufacturers such as Parent et Cie was to combine the technology of modern industry with the particular skill of French artisans, the production of luxury goods. The legacy of Parent et Cie has been preserved in eighty monumental volumes containing a sample of every button marketed by the company during the height of its productivity, from the 1860s to the 1880s. The over 80,000 buttons in the Parent sample books present an encyclopedic array of the artisan techniques known at the time. Included in the assortment are buttons of enamel, pearl, fabric, glass, papier-mâché, and endless varieties of metal—all could be produced in quantity and hand-finished, with variously and beautifully executed designs.

By mid-century, the variety of styles and techniques in the buttonmaking industry was astounding; technology made possible the processing of more kinds of materials and the creation of a greater variety of styles in more places than ever

Papier-mâché, French, mid-19th century

The term "lacquered" has come to describe the highly polished appearance produced by multiple layers of varnish; true lacquer, however, comes from the resin of certain Asian trees. These French papier-mâché buttons were made by a process of synthetic lacquering that was developed around 1800. The Oriental motifs may well be Western imitations of figures on authentic lacquered backgrounds.

*Papier-mâché, French,
mid-19th century*

This mesmerizing page of papier-
mâché lacquer buttons is from one of
eighty monumental French samples
books, containing over 80,000 buttons, acquired from the family of the
last owners of Albert Parent et Cie,
in 1984. The company was founded
in Paris in 1825 and remained the
foremost manufacturer of luxury
buttons into the early twentieth century. Parent et Cie kept a numbered
sample of each new design it produced. The buttons were mounted
on marbleized paper in bound
leather volumes with heavy brass
hinges. Still in mint condition, the
buttons—of enamel, pearl, fabric,
lacquer, and metals—were pro-
tected from the vagaries of time by
padded chintz sheets inserted between the pages. The significance of
this collection lies in its encyclopedic
documentation of the production of
buttons from 1825 to 1890.

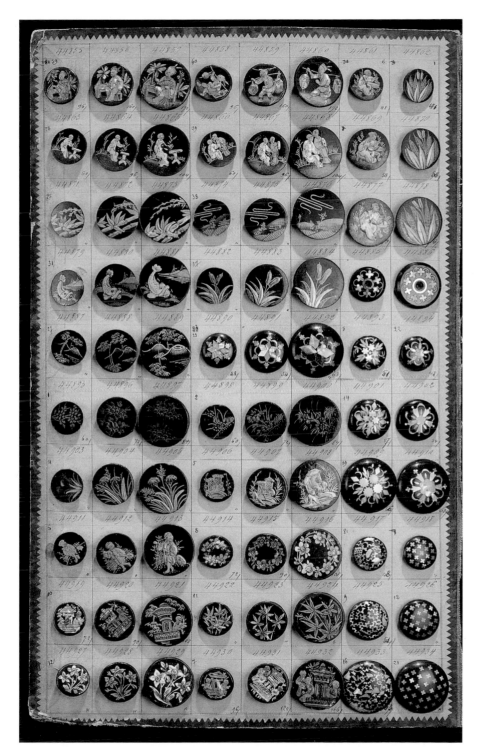

before. In many instances, these new technologies allowed for greater exploitation of materials or methods that had already been in use for centuries. Horn, for example, entered the utilitarian button market in the mid-nineteenth century only as the result of a method of commercial processing that allowed every bit of the horn to be powdered, compressed, and heated in molds. Similarly, shell buttons, which had been made by hand probably since the Renaissance, were produced in large quantities using machine methods from mid-century on, although sometimes at the expense of earlier standards of quality. Cameos, as well as buttons with pierced openwork patterns; with engraved, painted, or printed designs; and trimmed with escutcheons, pastes, or cut steels can be found from this period in a variety of shells, ranging in color from white through deep orange or tawny red to coffee-brown.

The button industry also began to use new synthetic materials in the late nineteenth century. Celluloid, the first of the synthetic plastics, was used first as a substitute for glass on lithograph buttons in the 1870s and then as a primary structural material, made to imitate ivory, horn, tortoiseshell, marble, and even

(opposite)
Celluloid, English, late 19th to early 20th century

Celluloid was developed commercially in the 1870s as a substitute for the ivory in billiard balls and was often made to imitate ivory in buttonmaking as well as in the manufacture of other small decorative objects. This striking group of buttons has incised and pigmented patterns and faceted steel accents. The curvilinear designs recall the fin-de-siècle work of such artisans as Aubrey Beardsley and Hector Guimard.

Tintypes, American, ca. 1860–1900

Tintypes, also known as "ferrotypes," are another example of nineteenth-century technologies applied to buttonmaking. Popular from the 1860s until the turn of the century, tintype buttons provided an inexpensive, portable form of portraiture and were worn by soldiers in the Civil War as mementos. The same photographic process was used at the time to produce political campaign buttons.

coral and jade. Other innovations were even more novel. The tintype, for example, was used by the button industry soon after its invention in the 1840s; tintype buttons served as tiny portable keepsake portraits from the 1860s to the early 1900s.

Fashions in the second half of the century helped to create a market for the new wealth of buttons. Men's clothes continued to manifest what the historian of dress J. C. Flugel has called "the great masculine renunciation"; color, cut, and materials were ever more moderate and increasingly standardized. The rich and colorful buttons of the eighteenth-century coat found no place on these antecedents of the modern business suit, and only the small glass or jewel buttons sometimes worn on vests betrayed faint traces of the former dazzle of men's costumes. At the same time, the role of display and conspicuous consumption fell to women. With the help of new aniline dyes, women's clothing became brighter and more visible amid the gray and crowded city streets; dresses became fancier and more ornamented as the century progressed.

Perhaps because of this emphasis on ostentatious display, buttons for women's clothing began more and more to resemble brooches and other decorative jewels. In fact, to a great extent the techniques and styles of women's fancy buttons in the second half of the century overlap or closely parallel those of contemporary jewelry. For the most part buttons made for women were larger and more ornate than the ones of fabric, gilt, and semiprecious stones that had been popular up through the 1850s. Enamel, porcelain, pearl, silver, and jeweled buttons met the Victorian demand for color, glitter, and variety.

The opening of trade with Japan in the 1850s began an encounter between East and West that was to have a tremendous influence in shaping European aesthetics. Japanese exports to the West allowed Europeans and Americans to experience objects firsthand that in the past had been jealously guarded. In 1862 Japanese artifacts were shown for the first time at the International Exhibition in London to a rapt public; in the 1870s, in Paris, there followed an unprecedented flow of such exotic accoutrements as samurai swords, embroidered silks, ornamented boxes, and jeweled and sculpted dagger cases. The artistic avant-garde, the Impressionists in particular, had already begun to challenge the academic conventions that had guided Western aesthetics since the Renaissance, and the introduction of Japanese aesthetics had a profound influence on Western art.

The manifestations of Japanese influence were varied, and buttons in the last decades of the nineteenth century evince many of them. Beginning around the 1870s, there appeared extraordinary Japanese buttons of ivory, pottery, and metal, many depicting traditional Japanese legends or bearing the spare, fragile floral or animal motifs typical of Japanese prints and pottery design. Since traditional Japanese costume did not require button fasteners, these were proba-

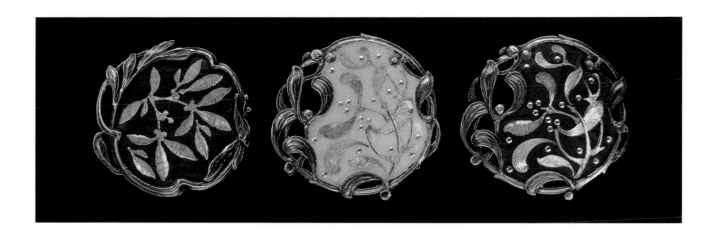

(above)
Enamel, French, late 19th century

Art Nouveau was heavily influenced by Japanese aesthetics, as these buttons illustrate: The asymmetry and stylized movement of natural form are both inspired by Japanese design. Gold-foil cutouts over enameled ground produce the mistletoe and laurel motifs; the silver borders repeat the leaf patterns.

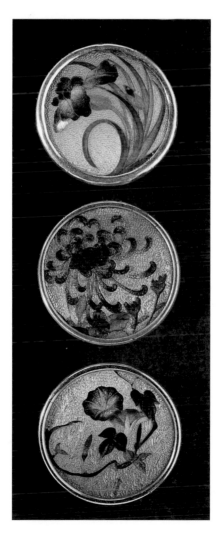

(opposite)
Enamel and silver, Japanese, late 19th century

Buttons such as these repoussé silver-and-enamel flowers were popular Japanese export items at the turn of the nineteenth century. Their flowing forms were consistent with turn-of-the-century Art Nouveau style, which had been influenced by Japanese design.

Enamel, Japanese, late 19th century

Japanese enameling blossomed after the first quarter of the nineteenth century. By mid-century, expertise in the technique allowed for innovations in fine cloisonné and crackle glaze. These buttons were produced in the late nineteenth century for export. The flowers, framed by a silver border, are set on a textured foil ground with a final layer of transparent enamel.

81

bly produced solely for Western consumption. Frequently, though, Japanese-looking buttons are the work of Western buttonmakers, whose designs of scenes and figures were sometimes imaginative imitations of those on actual articles from the East; many of the lacquer buttons from the latter part of the century fall into this category.

Finally, the principles of Japanese design—its spareness, asymmetry, and flowing lines—fundamentally influenced Art Nouveau and the many buttons that were designed in that style. Samuel Bing of Paris, Louis Comfort Tiffany of New York, and Arthur Lasenby Liberty of London were among the prominent promoters of the Art Nouveau style; their visits to Japan were vigorously encouraged by the Japanese government.

Matching, in fact surpassing, "japoniste" buttons in international appeal were the representational buttons produced in America, France, Austria, Germany, and England, and which reached their peak of popularity between 1870 and 1914. Buttons with pictorial designs had, of course, been in vogue since the late eighteenth century. Those referred to by collectors as "picture buttons," however, are peculiar to the late nineteenth century in several respects. Unlike the individually wrought buttons of the eighteenth century, the vast majority were mass-produced in metal, with the pictorial design either stamped or cast, usually in brass or cheaper metals. The two-part construction of most picture buttons meant that often the same design appears with different mountings. Whereas prints and paintings provided the imagery for many pictorial designs, the enormous scope of subject matter shown on picture buttons reflects, in part, the unprecedented quantity of printed matter available in the late nineteenth century. Motifs were lifted from every possible source, including an array of contemporary illustrations and trade cards. Nineteenth-century photographs and advertising announcements suggest that the primary selling point of picture buttons was the variety and interest of their designs and that they were frequently worn in a purely decorative manner. In any event, their artistic value is often less than that of other buttons of the period.

Picture buttons themselves embraced the Victorians' vast range of obsessions—from popular entertainments to historical or mythological figures, from birds and insects to real and imaginary animals, and every subject from anchors to signs of the zodiac. The appearance of several comets in the late nineteenth century probably provoked the rash of lyrical man-in-the-moon buttons, many with shooting stars, that appeared at the time. When in 1889 Gustave Eiffel's thousand-foot pylon broke into the Paris skyline, a variety of postcard-like views celebrated the appearance of the great tower. And, just as buttons commemorated the first hot-air balloon ascensions by the Montgolfier brothers in 1783, so in the late nineteenth century they celebrated bicycles, trains, and automobiles.

Pearl, French, late 19th century

These depictions of the Eiffel Tower display varying degrees of perspectival and topographical accuracy, but all three convey the profound visual impact of the thousand-foot iron pylon on the Parisian skyline. Commissioned for the centennial of the French Revolution in 1889, Gustave Eiffel's structure celebrated modern materials and engineering techniques and proclaimed the triumph of rationality, technology, and industrial progress in modern life. The mounted pearl button at far left bears the date of the tower's construction and may have been produced especially for the 1889 Exposition Universelle in Paris. The button on the far right humorously depicts a dandy of the eighteenth century examining the structure.

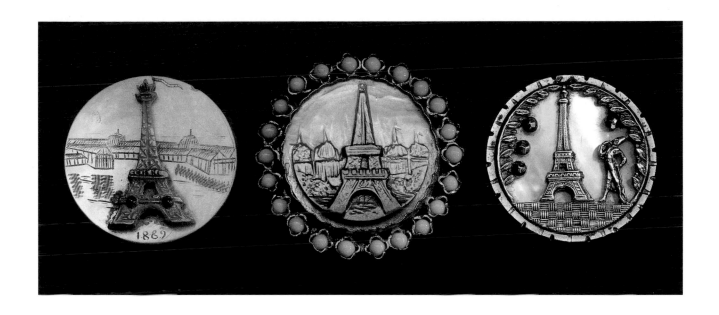

Mother-of-pearl, French, late 19th century

The imaginative use and juxtaposition of materials make these buttons noteworthy. The motif in the top center button is inlaid abalone shell with gilt decoration; the buttons at left and right are carved to show the layers of natural shading in the shell. The bottom row illustrates different combinations of shell and metalwork.

The popularity of storybook themes and nursery rhymes on picture buttons highlights another Victorian cult, that of the child. Attitudes toward children changed markedly from the mid-eighteenth century on, as childhood began to be perceived as a state distinct in all ways from adulthood. In the early nineteenth century, Romantic artists took the child as a symbol for the irrational and primitive impulses to which they themselves sought access. In the paintings of the German artist Philipp Otto Runge, robust, energetic children appear as untamed beings who belong as much to the natural world of the animals, trees, and flowers that surround them as they do to the rationalized human world. Similar sentiments about the primal link between children and nature are expressed in the pictorial designs on buttons of the same period.

The work of the British book illustrator Kate Greenaway perhaps best conveys the greater sentimentality and restraint of late-nineteenth-century approaches to the child. Greenaway's books began to appear in 1879 and met with remarkable success, not only in her own country but in America and on the Continent as well—and her pictures very quickly became a favorite source for button designs. Greenaway's well-behaved children are beautiful abstractions of Art Nouveau line and pastel coloring.

(opposite)
Various materials, late 19th to early 20th century

Kate Greenaway's garlanded children in country settings were an overwhelming success with the Victorian public and even earned the tempered praise of the famed nineteenth-century English art critic John Ruskin. It is not surprising, therefore, that many of the illustrations from her books and almanacs found their way onto buttons, or that these are a particular favorite among collectors. This assorted group of metal, ivory, and mother-of-pearl buttons includes identifiable Greenaway designs and probably a number of Greenaway-inspired figures as well.

Ceramic, probably English, late 19th century

Their decorative lines and playful associations made running geese a popular motif among late-nineteenth-century illustrators. These ceramic buttons recall the children's books of the English illustrator and craftsman Walter Crane. In 1875, tiles decorated with Crane's designs were sold in leading London stores. Blank tiles were also sold with the recommendation that the purchaser decorate them based on Crane's picture books. These anonymously produced buttons may have been decorated in a similar manner.

The pervasive use of black glass is another phenomenon that characterizes buttonmaking in the Victorian era. The death of her beloved husband, Prince Albert, in 1861 threw Queen Victoria into a period of mourning that lasted unrelieved until her death in 1901. During that time the queen wore only black, including black buttons and jewelry. Moreover, her obsessive mourning affected the national cultural life, as evidenced by the proliferation of exalted images of widows in painting and prose and the widespread fashion for black accessories.

This general affirmation of royal grief was an immediate boon to the Whitby jet industry. Jet is a form of fossilized driftwood found in the rocks along the Yorkshire coast near the fishing village of Whitby; it became the mourning stone of choice at court. Some extremely fine hand-fashioned jewelry and buttons were made in Whitby in the decades immediately following the Prince Consort's death. By the 1880s, however, jet had been surpassed in popularity by black glass, which was cheaper and easier to mass-produce. These glass "imitations" are by far the most plentiful type of black button worn during the period. They were made mostly in the predominant glass centers—Venice, Bohemia, and Austria—although a number of European-trained Americans established glass-button firms in the United States in the late nineteenth century. Millions were made in a mind-boggling variety of patterns and pictorial designs.

The nineteenth-century fascination with memorabilia and relics is also captured in a remarkable and scarce group of English buttons. Early in the century, single eyes—painstakingly rendered on paper, ivory, or enamel, often by the leading miniaturists of the time—were worn as mementos of the deceased. Although most of these were mounted as brooches or clasps, in quietly ornamental frames, exquisite buttons bearing the single-eye motif do appear. They are, in fact, among the century's most chillingly beautiful buttons.

In the last decades of the nineteenth century, button design reflected the desire to reconcile modern modes of production with earlier craft traditions. In England, William Morris's anti-industrial philosophy became the basis for the tremendously influential Arts and Crafts Movement, which, in turn, established the aesthetic basis of Art Nouveau in its many variations and incarnations. Rejection of the machine and a revived appreciation for organic form and the visible marks of craftmanship were the common stylistic feature of Continental, British, and American Art Nouveau, even though national differences inflected the products of each. The refuge from modern life that Art Nouveau invoked was only a respite, however. Although curvilinear designs and women with flowing hair appeared on buttons into the twentieth century, new developments in techniques and materials were soon to make them seem like relics from the past.

Etching, early 19th century

Eyes, eerily isolated and painstakingly rendered, were often worn as mourning jewelry in the early nineteenth century; some of the leading miniaturists of the period were engaged in the creation of these soulful mementos. These buttons are appropriately somber for mourning and reveal, even in their similarity, a remarkable variation and individuality.

The second and third buttons are bordered in marcasite.

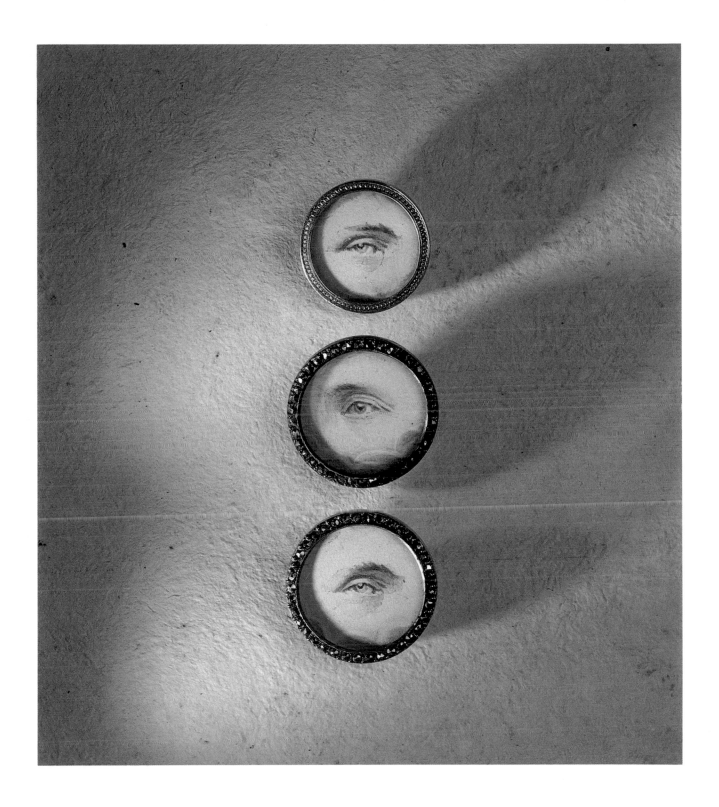

Enamel, early 19th century

This very fine painted-enamel button probably depicts a scene from the classical myth of the Lapiths and the Centaurs. According to the story, a terrible battle broke out at the wedding of Peirithous, king of the Lapiths, when the Centaurs, having had too much to drink, began carrying off the women. In this exceptional button, movement, color, and attention to detail are extraordinary; note the laces on the sandals; the water, rocks, trees; and the musculature of the Centaur's chest. (enlarged)

Enamel, French, mid-19th century

In the early nineteenth century, the excavations at Herculaneum and Pompeii had a strong impact on many of the decorative arts. This rare French grisaille enamel button depicts a grotesque mask. The finely drawn design and exacting use of white enamel, delineating features and shadows, attest to its superb quality.

Enamel, English and French mid to late 19th century

The eighteenth- and nineteenth-century fondness for Cupids, cherubs, and putti is clear from the plethora of buttons that depict them. This collection of buttons in assorted enamel techniques illustrates Neoclassical and Victorian treatments of this popular theme. The top center button is mounted in gold.

Enamel, probably French, early to mid-19th century

These are particularly beautiful examples of grisaille enamel painting, where white enamel has been applied thickly in parts to suggest sculptural relief and more sparingly elsewhere to allow the dark ground to show through. Here deep cobalt and molten red provide a striking contrast to the bisque-white, antique-inspired Cupid motifs.

*Enamel, French, mid to late
19th century*

Typical of nineteenth-century period re-
vivalism, these colorful buttons depict
eighteenth-century pastoral scenes. Of
special interest, in the bottom row, are
the refined polychrome-painted buttons
of wistful, languid young men.

Enamel, French, mid-19th century

The spirit of eighteenth-century Rococo
clearly lies behind these mid-nineteenth-
century scenes of playful children in
pastoral settings. These exquisite enamel
buttons have green basse-taille enamel
borders overset with a gilded baroque leaf
border; translucent peach enameling on
the reverse sides enhances the
quality of the set.

Enamel, French, ca. 1875

The pastoral figure of a shepherdess was a favorite image and a popular theme for fancy-dress entertainments throughout the eighteenth and nineteenth centuries. This button has an asymmetrical multi-colored champlevé border, enhanced by an outer border of semidetached paste. (enlarged)

Enamel, French, mid to late 19th century

During the Victorian period Cupid, the mythological god of love, was often represented as a playful, cherubic infant. These buttons showing Cupids and cherubs engaged in various amusements exemplify this theme and the sentimental notions of love it reveals.

(left)
Enamel, French, ca. 1875

The technique for polychrome painting on enamel, known as "émaux peints," was introduced in France at the beginning of the seventeenth century. In these nineteenth-century examples, colorful enamel designs of popular and playful pastimes are painted onto a background built up of successive layers of ground opaque glass. The surrounds are cut steel.

(right)
Enamel, French, ca. 1875

In the late nineteenth century an entertainment industry arose to meet the demands of an increasingly wealthy and powerful middle class. These French painted-enamel buttons with cut-steel borders refer to some of the ways and places in which the bourgeoisie spent their leisure hours. The buttons at top and second from the bottom depict Columbine and a clown, two figures of great popularity at the time; the second and bottom buttons show the specialized fashions that accompanied activities such as cycling and bathing.

Enamel and cut steel, French, ca. 1875

Fashion extremism in late-eighteenth-century France was a response to the sobriety of the Revolutionary period. These enamel buttons with cut-steel borders caricature the flamboyance of these men and women, known respectively as "incroyables" and "merveilleuses." Because of their outrageous sartorial habits, which included tight trousers and transparent gowns, "incroyables" and "merveilleuses" remained popular stereotypes decades after their costumes and mannerisms had become unfashionable. (enlarged)

Enamel, French, mid-19th century

The bucolic landscape scenes on these mid-nineteenth-century enamel buttons are characteristic of the Romantic fascination with nature. However, the black-and-white approach is distinctive, and the detailed and painterly rendering is exceptional. All have cut-steel borders.

(opposite)
Porcelain, various countries, mid-19th to 20th century

Each of these porcelain buttons bears the mark of the maker on the back, which is rare and of particular interest to the collector. For instance, the typical Dutch ship in underglaze blue is marked "Delft" on the reverse; the button at left, a stylized leaf pattern on a pale green ground, is marked "Minton" and is executed in the pâte-sur-pâte technique, which was developed by the Minton company in the mid-nineteenth century; the two buttons at bottom with blue-and-gold borders and delicate floral motifs are marked "Wedgwood" and probably date from the early twentieth century; the button at center with a hand-painted Gordon setter is an early-twentieth-century example of Wemyss ware and is extremely rare.

(above)
Porcelain, probably French,
late 19th century

These brilliantly colored porcelain buttons, with transfer-printed designs, bring together the motif of the four seasons with a particularly nineteenth-century preoccupation: the duties and pleasures of childhood.

(below)
Enamel, European, late 19th century

The painterly quality of these buttons bespeaks the sophisticated enameling techniques employed. The long, flowing hair and sixteenth-century costume suggest the broad influence of the English Pre-Raphaelites, who in the 1850s encouraged the medievalizing tendency in painting.

(opposite above)
Painting on ivory, French,
early 19th century

The late eighteenth century is notorious for flamboyant and short-lived hat styles. These buttons, set in silver mounts, illustrate a variety of headgear from the 1780s and convey something of the highly subtle nuances of hat-wearing at the time. Not only the style, but the position in which the hat was worn—for instance, flat or tilted to the back or side—was dictated by fashion.

(opposite below)
Porcelain, probably French,
early to mid-19th century

These glazed ceramic buttons, with transfer-printed designs and hand-painted gold accents, depicting animals and classical heads, were probably made in France. The heads reflect a fascination with classical themes; the animals in the top row are relatively rare. The buttons pictured are polychromatic on black and magenta backgrounds and are mounted in brass.

These painted porcelain buttons mimic, more or less closely, earlier portrait styles. In particular, the costumed woman at top resembles the portraits of the eighteenth-century painter Vigée-Lebrun; the subjects of the three middle buttons are derived from Italian Renaissance painting. The masked head at bottom has a paste border.

(right)
Various materials, French, 19th century

These buttons feature exceptional borders, or "frames." At top, an unusual brass Art Nouveau figure embraces a more staid-looking paste-bordered lithograph portrait; second from the bottom, a painting on ivory is set within a handsome striped border of pearl and brass inlay; the Gothic-looking woman and the shell cameo have especially lovely paste borders.

*Paintings on ivory, French,
early 19th century*

The painting in these buttons is especially
skillful, making them seem like true miniature portraits. In addition, the ornate
gilded-silver-and-pearl borders are meant
to recall late-eighteenth-century wooden
frames, which were often carved and
gilded to look like wrought metal.

*Painting on ivory, probably French,
early 19th century*

These ivory buttons, under glass with decorative silver mountings, exemplify the
delicate refinement of the Rococo. The
flower seller reveals a sentimental vision of
working-class life, but the woman in her
sumptuous interior reflects the ideal
of bourgeois leisure.

*Painting on ivory, Indian,
mid-19th century*

These ivory-and-silver-mounted buttons from India reveal the influence of European taste on Indian miniature painting. With the rise of British imperialism in the late eighteenth century, the traditional Mughal style, which had existed since the mid-sixteenth century, gave way to an offshoot known as the Company Style, after the East India Company. Typical of this style were depictions of the great monuments of India rendered in Western-inspired perspective and, especially in the nineteenth century, often painted in the chemical dyes that were produced by the British and which replaced the more mellow tones of previous generations.

(opposite)
*Painting on paper and ivory,
early to mid-19th century*

Lavishly illustrated natural-history books proliferated from the eighteenth century on. The most important of these, the comte de Buffon's monumental *Histoire naturelle,* published from 1749 to 1804, established the balance between observation and artifice that seems to lie behind the beautiful yet somewhat staged renderings of the lion and elephant. The three buttons shown above are from the mid-nineteenth century. All are under glass and mounted in brass.

Painting on ivory, early to mid-19th century

The combination of finely detailed birds and fairy-tale landscapes creates a particularly striking effect in these painted-ivory buttons in silver mounts under beveled glass.

(opposite)
Mother-of-pearl, French, mid to late 19th century

Production of white mother-of-pearl decreased in the second half of the nineteenth century as the importation of shell with darker and deeper lusters from Venezuela, Ceylon, Japan, and New Caledonia increased. This group of buttons features these darker shells, embellished by metal escutcheons, cut-steel trim, and decorative borders.

Mother-of-pearl, French, mid to late 19th century

These buttons illustrate the quality and variety of techniques used to produce carved-shell buttons in the second half of the nineteenth century. The fan, an almost mandatory Victorian accessory, is etched and pigmented with gold and silver. The center and bottom buttons use layered carving and double-mounted pearl to achieve the effect of Italian cameos, which were popular at the time.

*Mother-of-pearl, French, late
19th century*

The late-nineteenth-century fascination with exotic and unusual animals is evident in the choice of animals on these buttons. The realistically shaped carvings of the lion and owl, the use of glass eyes in the owl, and the pearl-in-pearl inlay of the bird are all atypical.

Abalone shell, French, late 19th century

These buttons feature popular motifs of the late nineteenth century, ranging from the ideal to the real. The center button marks the introduction of railroad travel, a fairly recent development that was greatly facilitated by viaducts like the one shown.

(opposite)
Inlay, English, mid to late 19th century

These buttons, often called "inlay," are particular favorites, primarily because of their graphic geometric patterns. The technique of applying veneers, or thin layers of iridescent abalone shell, tortoiseshell, ivory, and horn, was used to decorate the surfaces of many small objects in the mid- to late nineteenth and early twentieth centuries. Although they were inexpensive to produce, the contrast between the various materials creates an opulent visual effect.

Shell cameo, Italian and English (?), mid to late 19th century

The craft of shell carving enjoyed a renaissance beginning in the first decades of the nineteenth century, and cameos made from shells were in great demand throughout the Victorian period. The cameo buttons here, which span the century, suggest the reasons for their enormous popularity: their successful simulation of stone and the color variations achieved through the use of shells such as Queen's Conch, Black Helmut, and Bull's Mouth.

(opposite)

Tortoiseshell (piqué), English, ca. 1875

The decorations on these buttons were created by processes called "piqué point" and "piqué posé." In both techniques the tortoiseshell base is heated or soaked until malleable and then inlaid with silver or gold, which is secured when the shell dries. Piqué-point patterns consist of minute points of gold or silver level with the surface, while piqué posé uses strips of gold or silver to create scenes, designs, and geometric patterns. These buttons probably date from the last quarter of the nineteenth century, when hand piqué gave way to machine-made designs. This technique was more often used for jewelry, making these buttons all the more rare.

(left)
Tortoiseshell, English, ca. 1880

These unusual tortoiseshell buttons were made by pressing various inlay materials into a heated ground. At top, a wood marquetry band decorates a button set in a silver rim. The flowers and birds are abalone shell and silver, and the butterfly is etched and pigmented ivory.

(below)
Horn, probably English, late 19th century

Translucent horn, chosen for its resemblance to tortoiseshell, was used as the ground of this large button, inlaid with silver and brass. The standing heron, esteemed in the East for its calm attitude and grace, was a popular Chinese and Japanese decorative motif. Flecks of abalone are sprinkled at the bottom to add further luster. (enlarged)

Horn, English, ca. 1855

This bird is clearly depicted with an eye toward its romantic connotations. The dove and envelope are ivory inlaid in horn, with abalone shell and metal bits in the flowers below.

Inlay, English, mid-19th century

Inlaid decorations on horn and tortoiseshell buttons such as these are made by pressing the inlay material into the heated and thus malleable surface. The stylized bird and specimen insects on these buttons are made out of abalone shell and metal.

(above)
Horn, French, late 19th century

These unusual examples of French molded-horn buttons seem to have been painted by the same artist. The realistic and fantastic animals are inlaid with abalone shell and have gold and colored-paint accents.

*Brass, probably French, late
19th century*

Given their innate theatricality, it is perhaps not surprising that picture buttons such as these were often worn for decorative instead of utilitarian purposes. The design on the second button from top has been traced to a Currier & Ives print, *Skating in Central Park;* the depiction of Esmeralda and her dancing goat on the button below it derives from *Esmeralda,* an operatic adaptation of Victor Hugo's *Notre Dame de Paris.* The two remaining buttons are known, less precisely, as the "Skater" and the "Piano Player."

*Brass, probably French, late
19th century*

The stories in these metal buttons, whose designs probably date from the late nineteenth century, are told by the iconic portraits themselves. Clockwise from top left: a Pierrot with conventional neck ruff; possibly a child in a Napoleonic bonnet; an allegory of the South Wind; the goddess Athena; and a Kate Greenaway–like child.

Various metals, French and English, mid to late 19th century

Buttons with pictorial designs have been made in many periods and of many materials, but those known by collectors as "picture buttons" came into vogue in the second half of the nineteenth century and are usually metal with stamped or cast designs. This sampling of typical buttons suggests the variety of sources for the images, including contemporary illustrations, trade cards, and a wide range of literary works.

Brass, probably French, late 19th century

Each of these picture buttons is notable for its beautifully crafted border. The handkerchief folds on the middle-left button were a favorite nineteenth-century conceit and, as in this example, were usually made by placing one metal square diagonally over another to produce eight corners. The buttons on the left and right are decorated with cut steel.

*Mother-of-pearl, English,
early to mid-19th century*

The equestrian motifs on these sporting buttons are etched in mother-of-pearl and pigmented in a manner similar to that used on ivory, most notably in scrimshaw.

*Mother-of-pearl, English,
mid-19th century*

These buttons, engraved with coaching scenes, are similar in spirit to the sporting buttons that were worn by hunting enthusiasts in the early part of the century. Coaching was a popular English gentleman's sport of the time, and the coachmen were said to have worn large pearl buttons on the capes of their uniforms. As with sporting buttons, these may have belonged to a participant or simply a viewer of the sport.

Enamel, French, probably mid to late 19th century

The enthusiasm for outdoor sports and for buttons with sporting subjects coincided, not surprisingly, with the growth of cities and of a population increasingly nostalgic for the country life. This magnificent and very rare set of silver and basse-taille enamel buttons may have been worn by a follower of the hunt, but it may just as likely have been made for the silk or satin coats of an urban aristocrat. The back mark is "A. Bagniot Paris."

Brass, French, mid to late 19th century

These double-mounted sporting buttons all bear French maker's marks. The various game animals are silver escutcheons attached to brass backs. The detailing, high relief, and solid construction attest to their fine quality.

Various materials and countries, 19th century

Crescent and full-faced moons—made of carved pearl, ivory, and silver—reflect the popularity of the subject in the nineteenth century. Two of the most poetic examples are the carved ivory button at top and, right, the silver-plated commedia dell'arte character Scaramouche gazing at the moon through vaporous clouds.

Brass, French, late 19th century

The moon appears with conventional iconography in these metal buttons: with a rooster at left, and at center, with a man brushing off cobwebs. The remaining three buttons show the commedia dell'arte character Scaramouche, who serenaded Columbine from a crescent moon in the traveling shows of the late nineteenth century.

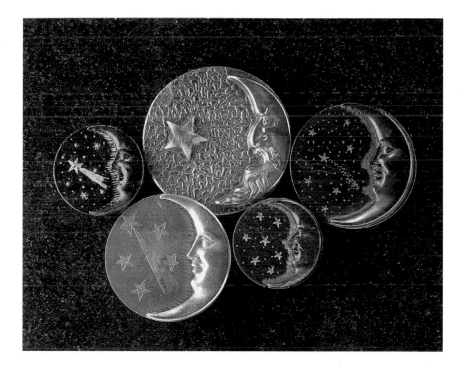

Brass, French, late 19th century

The transformation of the moon and stars from symbols with mythical or religious content to anecdotal, sentimental figures is reflected in these buttons. They feature crescent men-in-the-moon and comets, which were seen frequently and with some excitement at the time; the textured brass button at top presents an unusually animated profile.

*Various materials, probably French,
late 19th century*

The realistic detail of these brass dog buttons conveys both the physical appearance and the personality traits of three favorite breeds: from left to right, a whippet decorated with cut steel, a boxer on a pearl ground, and a barrel-toting St. Bernard on a cut-steel ground.

*Various materials and countries,
mid-19th to early 20th century*

Their presence in daily life and their real or imagined similarities to human behavior make dogs a favorite modern subject, especially for the decoration of everyday objects such as buttons. This assortment reveals the sentimentalizing and humanizing tendency that has characterized Western attitudes toward dogs since the early nineteenth century.

(above)
Brass, probably French, late 19th to early 20th century

Each of the designs on these picture buttons has its source in a popular children's story. From left to right they depict: the Little Colonel from an 1895 children's book of the same name; Buster Brown, the protagonist in Richard Outcault's comic strip from 1902 to 1920; the Little Tailor of nursery-tale fame; Little Red Riding Hood and the Wolf; and Johnny and the Vine, a design from Kate Greenaway's *Under the Window.*

Metal, Japanese, 19th century

Although these "buttons" were not originally used as fasteners for garments, they are prized and collected. Known as "kagagami-buta," they were the centerpieces of round netsukes known as "manjū." Manjū netsukes—made from carved wood, ivory, or horn—were worn over a man's obi sash as a counterweight for a money purse or tobacco case, the two being connected by a chain or silk cord. Decorated in low relief, etched, engraved, and embellished with gold, silver, and other precious metals, these bronze "buttons" are exceptional examples of Japanese metalwork, known as "shakudo," a skill historically devoted to the revered craft of sword making.

Satsuma, Japanese, late 19th century

The beauty of these buttons is matched by their symbolic richness. The opulent patterns at top incorporate traditional motifs: the thousand cranes, symbolizing longevity; the chrysanthemum, representing autumn; and birds in a moonlit blossoming tree, an allusion to haiku poetry. The bottom row features more realistic elements: insects, household objects, and a reference to the Japanese navy.

Satsuma, Japanese, late 19th century

These dramatic, heavily gilded Satsuma buttons depict a variety of mythical and everyday Japanese characters. The goldfish in the button at lower left identifies the male figure as one of the seven deities, known as "Daikokuten," a symbol of good luck and happiness.

(above)
Ivory, Japanese, mid to late
19th century

This set of Shibayama ivory buttons with fragile inlaid floral designs was brought back from the Orient and resold in a European presentation box. This practice was common among nineteenth century jewelers.

Satsuma, Japanese, late 19th century

Although kilns were established in Satsuma, a former province of Japan, in the early seventeenth century, the Satsuma ware produced for export was first introduced to the West at the Exposition Universelle in Paris in 1867. The pottery is characterized by a crackle glaze and an overglaze of polychrome painting with heavily encrusted gilding. The borders in these buttons are especially interesting. At top, a rich cobalt underglaze gilded with a geometric pattern encircles a geisha; at bottom, a similar underglaze beneath a seaweed design frames two irises; and at center, the trefoil border echoes the forms and colors of the butterfly.

The eighteenth-century Japanese netsuke carver Shibayama gave his name to the distinctive style of encrusted inlay employed on these late-nineteenth- or early-twentieth-century ivory buttons. These naturalistically posed birds are inlaid with semiprecious jade, coral, and pearl shell.

(opposite)

Ivory, Japanese, late 19th to early 20th century

The lozenge shapes enhance the "peephole" effect of these intimate views of a pair of rabbits on these captivating etched ivory buttons. Although they lack any definitive identifying marks, the unconventional designs and the delicacy of their execution suggest that these buttons were produced in Japan, probably in the late nineteenth to early twentieth century. (enlarged)

(opposite)
Ivory, Alaskan, mid-19th to early 20th century

These carved Eskimo ivory "portraits" depict walruses, and probably a seal at top. The touches of red pigment in the middle two buttons are an unusual feature.

Ivory, Alaskan, mid-19th to early 20th century

This mixed group shows Eskimo buttons and toggles in walrus ivory with etched and pigmented decorative patterns. In some instances, the nose and eyes have been inset with baleen, a black ivory taken from the whalebone whale. Although highly stylized, these animal shapes demonstrate the carvers' remarkable ability to convey recognizable features with just a few marks and cuts. The Eskimos believe that each piece of ivory possesses a form that is released by the carver.

Ivory, Alaskan, early 20th century

These etched Eskimo ivory buttons were probably tailored to the tastes and demands of visitors to Alaska in the early part of the twentieth century. The depictions of Eskimos in native costume would have served as ideal souvenirs for American and European miners and sailors.

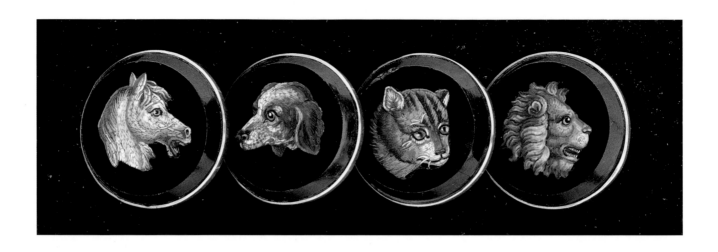

(opposite)
Mosaic, Italian, late 19th century

These exceptional animal-head micro-mosaic buttons on black-glass grounds, in gilt mountings, exemplify the high-quality craftsmanship of the mosaic workshops in Italy during the last quarter of the nineteenth century. These workshops produced only the mosaics, which were then sold to local merchants and craftsmen who used them to decorate a variety of objects.

(opposite)
Pietra dura, Italian, mid-19th century

Here semiprecious stones such as chalcedony, agate, coral, and jasper are set on a base of black marble in a technique called "pietra dura" or "Florentine work." Since the stones' own tonalities suggest nature's shadows and coloration, the technique is especially suited to fruit and foliage motifs, as in these exquisite buttons in silver rope-border mountings.

Mosaic, Italian, mid-19th century

This micromosaic button depicts a finely detailed stone bridge and ruins. The gold frame and back enhance the high quality of the mosaic work.

Paste, French and English, 19th century

Although nineteenth-century pastes were appreciated in their own right, they were also used to simulate precious stones, especially diamonds. The development of flint glass, a colorless and highly refractive glass, is attributed to George Ravenscroft in 1675. But it is Georges Frédéric Strass, a Parisian jeweler in the early eighteenth century, who is credited with having vastly extended the range and quality of paste jewelry, and whose name is often used synonymously with it. The buttons pictured combine diamond-like paste stones with enamel in sumptuous designs; the two at lower right are set in gold, the rest in silver mountings.

Marcasite, French, mid-19th century

The vogue for diamond jewelry in the eighteenth century produced a demand for convincing substitutes, including marcasite. Although sometimes confused with faceted steel because of its metallic sheen, true marcasite, a crystallized form of iron pyrite, is very rarely found in buttons. The examples pictured reveal the intricate floral patterns that characterize marcasite buttons.

Aluminum, French, late 19th century

Although its current applications make it difficult to perceive as a precious metal, aluminum was introduced at the Paris Exposition Universelle in 1855 as an expensive novelty, and it remained highly valuable until the twentieth century, when new technologies made it cheaper to extract. The beautifully conceived, delicately stamped and chased floral designs on these buttons attest to their value. The three bottom buttons are aluminum made to imitate tortoiseshell.

*Glass, Czechoslovakian or Austrian,
late 19th to early 20th century*

"Lacy glass" is a collectors' term initially applied to these turn-of-the-century pressed-glass buttons because of their resemblance to the "lacy glass" produced by the Sandwich glassworks. Besides the molded patterns, what distinguishes lacy buttons from similarly textured ones is the paint applied to the back, which gives them their ethereal glow. Although most are made from clear glass, occasionally transparent colored glass was used in addition to the colored backing. These buttons are accented with silver and gold lusters.

Glass, French, ca. 1900

Both the organic motifs and the understated tones on these metal-mounted glass buttons reveal the influence of the Art Nouveau glass artist Emile Gallé, although they exude a calm and repose absent from most of Gallé's designs. The raised patterns are either molded or acid-etched; some of the metal backs bear the initials of Arthur Kim, a Parisian artisan known to have made buttons in ivory and enamel as well.

Silver, English and French, ca. 1900–1910

These English and French silver buttons, circa 1900 to 1910, feature
the typical Art Nouveau female face. The buttons are striking for
their sinuous shapes and vegetable forms, which seem to deny the
solidity of their material. This fantastic use of cast metal to evoke
an organic vision is characteristic of Art Nouveau objects.

Brass and silver plate, French, ca. 1895

The characteristic Art Nouveau profile is here combined with words and emblems representing the four elements—fire, air, water, earth—and the times of day—night, day, dawn, dusk. By the late nineteenth century, the Art Nouveau woman was a significant symbolic as well as decorative motif. In 1895, roughly the year these buttons were produced, the one-franc piece was redesigned by Oscar Roty with an image of Marianne, symbol of France, an agile young woman shown in profile, with flowing robes and cascading hair.

Silver, various countries, late 19th to early 20th century

Hallmarks and silver marks are to silver what signatures are to paintings: a means by which to identify the maker, date, and origin of the work. Hallmarks were introduced in the thirteenth century to ensure against the sale of inferior-quality silver; the term "hallmark" itself is said to derive from the Goldsmith's Hall, where, beginning in the fifteenth century, English workers were ordered to bring their wares to be assayed and marked. These buttons each bear a British or Continental hallmark, and in most instances the initials of the maker alongside an official mark.

Enamel, French and English,
ca. 1925

The flat geometric and interwoven shapes of Art Deco adapted well to the button format. Rejecting the flowing forms and delicate colors of Art Nouveau, Art Deco button-makers used angular motifs done in the strong enamel colors fashionable in the 1920s. Since the use of enameling began to lose popularity after the Art Nouveau period, these buttons are quite scarce.

he relationship of buttons to the speed and rhythm of modern life is captured aptly, if outrageously, in a scene from the 1936 film *Modern Times*. In a delirium induced by the assembly line, Charlie Chaplin, a huge wrench in each hand, chases after round buttons prominently displayed on the backs and bodices of nearby women's dresses in an attempt to "tighten" them.

In some respects, buttons seem out of step with the tempo of the twentieth century. The long rows of buttons that lined the basques of Victorian women connote a world of leisure, of slow, measured movement and manual dexterity. By contrast, the dynamism and mechanization of the early twentieth century are incarnated in an invention whose very name conjures up speeding cars and moving staircases: the zipper. Patented in 1893, the zipper, or "slide fastener," as it was initially called, achieved commercial success only in the 1930s, when its quick, easy motion was made the major point of promotion. In 1931 the Hookless Fastener Company claimed, "No longer is mother's day filled with the plaintive plea 'Button me, please!' Nowadays Talon fastened youngsters take pride in being able to dress themselves without help—three full years before the average buttoned baby is able to put on or take off a thing!"

In the first two decades of the twentieth century, buttons became simple, much as they had been at the beginning of the previous century. The growth of the white-collar class had as a corollary the emergence of the corporate look: sedate, standardized, and perfectly coordinated. Moreover, as the accented curves of women's clothing gave way to the more angular silhouette of man-tailored suits, buttons, too, began to lose their gender distinctions. The simple four-holed button, introduced into men's fashion around the turn of the century, became standard for women's blouses as well, and beginning after 1910, carded sets of inexpensive, generic buttons were sold in five-and-dime stores.

Buttonless dresses and costume jewelry further meant that, for a while at least, the demand for flamboyant, extravagantly wrought buttons was on the wane. The garter button was a notable exception to this trend; visible for the first time in the 1920s, satin buttons with ribbons and printed or painted designs were worn on stockings that came to just below the knee.

As if in response to the threat of the kinetic fastener, as the century progressed ever more novel and eccentric buttons began to emerge alongside commonplace ones. In the 1930s new synthetic materials made possible the most outrageous buttons since the extravagances of the eighteenth century. Bakelite, invented in 1907, had, by the early 1930s, almost completely replaced all other plastics in the production of trinkets and other accessories. Called the "material of a thousand uses," its success lay largely in its combination of durability and versatility: Bakelite could be sawed, sliced, ground, and carved into any number of shapes, and it came

Plastic, American, ca. 1930s

Plastic is used to striking effect in these rare inlaid Art Deco buttons from the 1930s. The clean, geometric patterns and organic color schemes reflect the style of Art Deco and create a subdued appeal. The fine orange strips that join the clear and opaque plastics add an extremely subtle visual refinement.

Brass and vegetable ivory, American, ca. 1930s–1940s

The innovation of giving the dwarfs individual and identifiable personalities was undoubtedly largely responsible for the overwhelming success of Walt Disney's 1937 film *Snow White and the Seven Dwarfs.* These scarce buttons reproduce members of the septet in all their cinematic appeal. Bashful and Dopey at top are stamped in brass; the dwarfs below appear on buttons of celluloid and vegetable ivory, a material made from the nuts of the corozo or tagua palms, and represent two differently colored sets.

in a wide range of vibrant, nonfading colors. The introduction, also in the early 1930s, of a product similar to Bakelite, but with an even greater capacity to hold color, further increased the aesthetic possibilities of plastic design. Catalin plastic, as the new product was trademarked, was available in over two hundred dazzling opaque, marbleized, translucent, and transparent varieties.

The potential of synthetic plastic was tremendous, and as always, the button industry was quick to take full advantage. On the one hand, Bakelite buttons in subdued colors and crisp geometric patterns captured the cool appeal of Art Deco. On the other hand, however, the bright colors and malleability of the material also spawned a seemingly limitless array of novelty buttons, shaped like the objects they were meant to represent and known as "realistics" or "goofies" by collectors.

The quest for novelty was, in fact, probably the motivating force behind the barrage of realistics produced in the 1930s and 1940s. Manufacturers, vying for a rapidly changing market, could draw upon practically any and every commonplace item as subject, and indeed, buttons began to reflect the wide variety of materials and objects in modern life, as they took the shapes of animals, telephones, bowling pins, martinis, sailors, and school supplies. In the 1930s the Catalin Corporation advertised a "Style-Fruit" line, a variety of succulent carved plastic apples, bananas, corn-on-the-cob, which were sold as buttons, earrings, bracelets, and necklaces. These were among the most popular novelty buttons of the period. Buttons in the shape of miniature cigarette boxes, with exact replicas of common brand-name wrappers, were popular through the 1940s.

In addition to providing endless variety to a demanding button market, the kaleidoscopic displays of buttons presented in the 1930s and 40s also offered a kind of relief during troubled times. Even in depression and war, clothes could glisten with fresh food and other consumer goods. Striking, emphatic buttons might also draw attention away from lesser-quality fabrics and designs. Sober wartime fashions could be brightened by colorful pieces of glass and plastic. During World War II, despite rationing and shortages, button manufacture actually increased in America, making do with whatever materials were available. In fact, acrylic left over from bomber-gun turrets was transformed into the delicate floral buttons that graced women's dresses and suits.

It was also in the second quarter of the century that buttons allied themselves with two important bastions of fantasy, Hollywood and the world of high fashion. The remarkable success of Walt Disney cartoons, for example, gave rise to a range of salable paraphernalia depicting favorite Disney characters, including buttons in the shapes of Minnie, Mickey, Donald Duck, and Snow White and the Seven Dwarfs. With the emergence of a generation of avant-garde designers who made the button a primary focal point, buttons of plastic, wood, and other inexpensive materials entered the world of haute couture. Elsa Schiaparelli, who probably did more than any other designer to reinstall the button as a flamboyant fashion element, used them prominently and outrageously on everything from bathing suits to formal wear.

As realistically shaped buttons celebrated the progress of the industrialized West by reproducing its products and icons, the search for preindustrial alternatives found expression in buttons that evoked the "primitive." Africa, a source of artistic inspiration for the Parisian avant-garde at the beginning of the century, became a source of fashion inspiration when socialites and heiresses began returning from their safaris laden with African trinkets. Shortly thereafter, wooden buttons carved like African human and animal heads, and buttons with African motifs, were brought home as souvenirs of travel. The same exotic wanderlust resulted in the appearance of Alaskan artifacts, among them, carved ivory buttons in the shapes of seals, walruses, whales, and fish, as well as buttons etched with pictorial scenes of Eskimo life.

Even more than in previous centuries, the introduction of inexpensive materials and mass-producible designs in the twentieth century has brought about a transformation of the button industry, especially in respect to the role of individual handicraft. As realistics demonstrated, machine-produced plastic buttons could almost recreate the enthusiasm and spirit, the variety and flair of the eighteenth century—and without expensive detailing or significant hand-touches. The growth of the plastics industry, in fact, probably contributed considerably to the demise of the inexpensive glass and pearl button by the 1960s.

Earlier in the century, efforts had been made to unite glassmaking with mass-production techniques. Makers of glass buttons often used simple molded or etched designs that could be reproduced in various colors in different mountings. By the latter part of the century, however, glass buttons, made by hand in uncomfortably hot factories under unpleasant conditions, could no longer compete with modern plastics. The number of glass factories in West Germany, the primary exporter of glass buttons after World War II, fell from over five hundred in 1952 to about fifty in 1969.

Other factors have limited the range of materials used in buttonmaking. For instance, natural materials such as tortoiseshell, elephant ivory, and whale ivory have been banned in the United States and other countries in recent years in order to protect the animals that are killed to obtain them.

The increased use of plastic and the absorption of buttonmaking by big industry notwithstanding, the interest in buttons as collectible artifacts has begotten a new type of handcrafted button in the twentieth century: the studio button. First produced in the 1930s, studio buttons cater to a burgeoning collectors' market and often are never worn. The collectors' interest has put a new premium on buttons

Paper, American, ca. 1950s–1960s

This three-dimensional television button of printed paper, mounted under glass, attests to the growth and popularity of button collecting in recent decades. Harry Wessel, the husband of an avid button collector, began making buttons in 1952 specifically as collectibles and not for wear or use. Other buttons in his repertoire include religious scenes, peacock feathers, political figures, and his grandchildren. Except for the very earliest examples, they are signed with an "HGW" on the back.

"Hat styles from the twentieth and twenty-first centuries" might humorously caption these otherwise wildly dissimilar heads. The sleek Dietrichesque button at left is made from German bisque glass with molded and hand-painted features and probably dates from the 1930s. The brass head at right is American and recalls the futuristic fantasies of the forties and fifties. (enlarged)

that bear the mark of an individual craftsman and are produced in small quantities.

Massachusetts glassblower Charles Kaziun, whose primary fame is in the field of highly collectible desk paperweights, is a pertinent example of a craftsman commissioned by button collectors, in the 1950s, to produce buttons in the manner of his larger works. Kaziun's exquisite miniature paperweight buttons are sought by collectors of both paperweights and buttons.

Buttons made out of a broad spectrum of materials, employing a vast range of techniques, have brought a renaissance to contemporary buttonmaking. As even a brief outline of button history suggests, the handcrafted or unique object is never obsolete. The sumptuously handwrought buttons of the eighteenth century, nineteenth-century craft-revival buttons, and twentieth-century studio buttons, among others, manifest a continuing appreciation for the button's aethestic and symbolic dimensions.

Buttons were, most likely, born out of an impulse for display, and the desire for self-expressive adornment continues to give rise to extraordinary and extravagant examples of the craft. The history of buttonmaking from the eighteenth century on is, after all, a narrative of cultural and historical assimilation and especially of the perpetual pursuit of the new and distinct. The momentum of that pursuit is still with us.

Enamel, French and English, early 20th century

These diverse buttons all employ an enameling technique known as "guilloché." This method first appeared in the mid-eighteenth century with the invention of the tour-à-guillocher, a machine that engraves metal in regular patterns. After the pattern is created, transparent or translucent enamel is applied to create a shimmering, luminous effect. In the nineteenth century, the technique was famously revived by the fine jeweler Fabergé. The blue-and-gold-foil enamel button (lower right), is signed "Cartier-Paris, Londres." The top three buttons are hallmarked gilded silver and are dated between 1903 and 1905.

Mosaic, Italian, early 20th century

European interest in Egypt, sparked by the Nile Valley excavations in the late 1860s, reached a peak with the discovery of Tutankhamun's tomb in 1923. These Italian glass micromosaic buttons probably date from the early twentieth century. The scarab motif was especially popular in this period, and although the workmanship does not match the complexity of true ancient Egyptian pieces, the iridescent colors capture some of the mesmerizing beauty of the originals. The oval button is in gold.

(opposite)

Satsuma, Japanese, mid-20th century

The development of Satsuma pottery from the late nineteenth to the mid-twentieth century reveals the influence of contact with the West. For instance, these large buttons with blue-tinged, gilded grounds adopt Western modeling techniques in the shadings on the trout and lobster. Fewer brushstrokes and less complex painting and detail reflect the deterioration in quality over time and firmly date these buttons.

Porcelain, English, early 20th century

These rare buttons are as unusual for the realism of their seascapes as for the detail of their maker's marks, which read "England, Coalport, A.D. 1750, V4875." Although founded in 1750, Coalport Porcelain began producing buttons only in the early twentieth century. Images such as those pictured here are typical of Coalport porcelains of this period and were probably designed by artists employed by the factory.

Silver and pewter, English, early 20th century

These silver and pewter buttons, with ceramic or stone center medallions, exemplify the early-twentieth-century English Arts and Crafts Movement. Under the leadership of William Morris, the movement sought to remedy the ill effects of modern industrial production through a return to medieval craft practices. Made in workshops, called "guilds," that specialized in handicrafts, they bear the hammered texture and hand-tooled look of medieval metalwork.

Silver, English, 1904

This is a matched set of silver and enamel buttons in the original box from the English firm Liberty & Co., marked "Birmingham, 1904, L & Co." The phosphorescent blue-and-green colors of the peacock became the predominant color scheme of the Liberty style.

Silver, English, ca. 1900

Taking their inspiration from the motifs of the Middle Ages, many designers of the English Arts and Crafts Movement assimilated Celtic design elements into their work. This style became synonymous with the firm Liberty & Co. Arthur Lasenby Liberty, a brilliant merchant with aesthetic sensibilities, commissioned artists, both known and unknown, to design and manufacture everyday objects. The designs of these hallmarked silver and enamel buttons, made between 1900 and 1904, can be seen on other small silver objects, such as napkin rings, matchbox holders, pillboxes, etc. The tree appears on Moorcroft pottery.

Silver, American, mid-20th century

These intriguing modernist buttons belonged to Nellie Parker Van Buskirk, an early-twentieth-century collector who commissioned them from various craftsmen in the course of her wide travels. With the exception of the unmarked serpentine button at top, each bears a different maker's mark. Talented as well as resourceful, Van Buskirk eventually became a silversmith in her own right and produced the round Jensen-like button at upper left.

(opposite)
Silver, Danish and American, 1st half of 20th century

The first three buttons are rare examples by the twentieth-century Danish silversmith Georg Jensen. Jensen opened his workshop in 1904, but it was his collaboration with, among others, the young painter Johan Rohde, beginning in 1906, that produced the distinctive look evident here. Their characteristic style, a balance between swelling, sensual lines and austere surfaces, was perpetuated under Jensen's name even after the deaths of both him and Rohde in 1935. The two lower buttons were made by American craftsmen in the 1940s, illustrating the far-reaching influence of the Jensen style.

Glass, probably French, early 20th century

Well constructed and finely executed, these buttons, mounted in brass, clearly show the influence and aesthetic appeal of the Art Nouveau style. The designs were outlined in gold on the back of the glass, filled in with black paint, and then set against an iridescent background of abalone shell.

Glass, French, early 20th century

What makes these molded-glass buttons unusually rare and valuable is the etched signature, "R. Lalique." René Lalique's determination to produce fine-quality objects using mass-production techniques led him to experiment with an enormous range of glass goods, including buttons. These buttons, probably from the 1920s, demonstrate Lalique's affinity for pure colors and clear glass and his tendency to rely on design to create an impact. The blue-glass button at top has a silver center; the wood nymphs, in red and delicate lavender, are set with semipearls and mounted in silver and include the words "Fioret Paris" next to the signature.

Enamel, probably French, ca. 1900

With the Art Nouveau and the Arts and Crafts movements in the nineteenth century came a revival of earlier enameling techniques, including plique-à-jour, the process used to create these buttons. In plique-à-jour, an open-patterned framework of metal is filled with multicolored transparent enamel to produce an effect similar to that of stained glass. Highly regarded and sought after by collectors, these buttons are fragile and very rare. The sedate geometric button at top employs a more refined version of the technique, in which the enamel is polished to a fine matte translucent finish.

(opposite)
Wood, African, mid-20th century

Serious Western interest in African art was sparked by experiments in abstraction in the early twentieth century. These carved teak and ebony buttons, probably from before World War II, demonstrate the visual aspects of African sculpture that attracted the Western avant-garde: simplified linear forms and a departure from strict imitation of natural appearances.

Silver, Navajo, early 20th century

These handsome silver and turquoise buttons are made to resemble round and oval conchs, or shells. This group displays a combination of stamped decoration and chiseling, as well as the more intricate repoussé technique. The button on the lower left is sand-cast. Although the earliest Navajo buttons were plain metal disks, the ornateness of these may reflect the increasingly ornamental role of buttons as Navajo women adopted Western-style dress.

(opposite)
Wood and ivory, African, mid-20th century

The choice of materials in these buttons is probably of more than simply aesthetic significance; it is said that to the African sculptor raw materials are invested with spiritual attributes prior to their transmutation into specific forms.

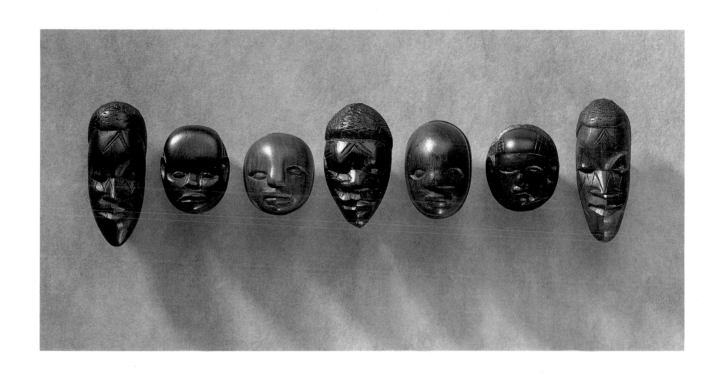

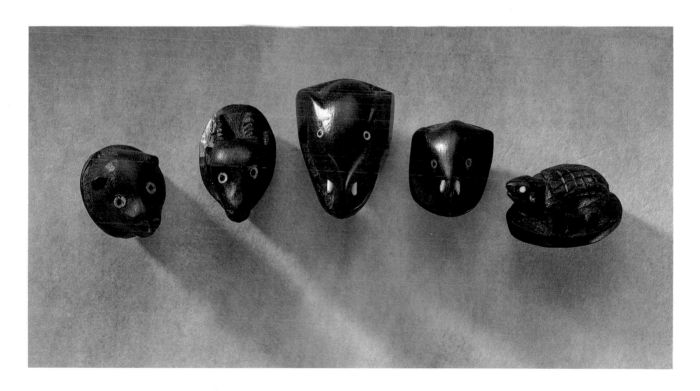

*Humorous button cards, American,
ca. 1920*

Cards from the 1910s and 1920s illustrate the various novelty uses for buttons. At left, real buttons add visual effect to a common and disparaging joke about women's quest for equal rights; in the valentine at center buttons stand in for the last word of a similarly antifeminist rhyme that contrasts "jazz gluttons" with proper, button-sewing women; the postcard at right uses a two-hole bone trouser button to represent the simplified face of a member of the button family.

*(opposite)
Carded buttons, American,
ca. 1930s–1940s*

Cards showing buttons "in situ" were sold in five-and-dimes beginning in the early twentieth century and were probably intended to add visual interest to store displays, as well as to give the buttons an aura of fashion. These handsome Hollywood types in shirtsleeves are depicted in brightly colored lithographs and date from the 1930s to 1940s.

Silk, American, early 20th century

Diminishing skirt lengths in the first decades of the twentieth century revealed heretofore hidden body parts and buttons. Decorated silk garter buttons were made for the fancy garters worn below the knee on the outside of stockings from about 1910 to 1930. The example pictured here is exceptional for the complete body formed out of laced ribbons.

Silk, American, ca. 1920s–1930s

These painted or printed American silk garter buttons bear the flapper features typified by such popular icons of the 1920s and 1930s as the movie actress Clara Bow and the cartoon character Betty Boop: small heart-shaped lips, Egyptian eyes, and bobbed hair. The policeman signaling "stop" hints at the vaguely erotic and risqué nature of these buttons.

Enamel, Indian, ca. 1940s–1950s

These enamel-on-silver buttons were executed by B. Motiwala, a Bombay artisan who produced a vast range of buttons on specification for American collectors in the 1940s and 1950s. The meticulously reproduced designs correspond to specific illustrations from Kate Greenaway's *Mother Goose* and *Birthday Book*.

(opposite)
Plastic, American, ca. 1940s

The relative simplicity of these clear plastic buttons with floral motifs, reverse-carved and painted, belongs more to the simpler styles of the 1940s than to the bold plastic patterns of the previous decade. The increased use of Lucite for buttons after World War II was probably the result of the availability of scraps and off-cuts from the United States government, which used Lucite for airplane cockpit canopies.

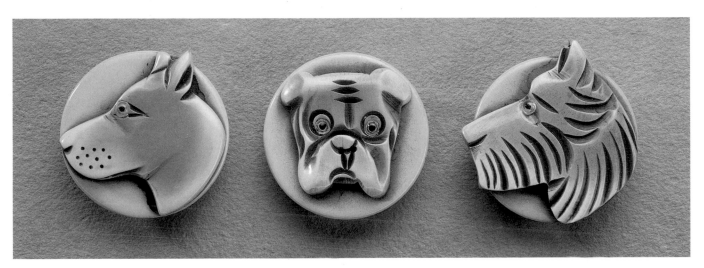

(opposite)
Plastic, American, ca. 1930s

Exuberant buttons such as these proliferated in the economically depressed 1930s
and provided an inexpensive and cheerful
form of ornament. These Bakelite buttons
in decorative abstract patterns are
typical of the period.

Plastic, American, late 1930s

The significance of the household dog as an emblem of the American life-style may explain its
popularity in the late 1930s as a motif on jewelry
and buttons. Franklin D. Roosevelt's pet Scottie,
Fala, was the national mascot of the period and the
inspiration for countless Scottie dog reproductions. These Bakelite buttons emulate the
look of carved ivory.

Plastic, American, ca. 1930s

By the early 1930s Bakelite had almost
completely replaced other plastics in the
production of fashion accessories. This
assortment of buttons from the thirties
illustrates some of the most visible reasons
for its popularity. Extremely versatile,
Bakelite lent itself to fantastic shapes and
designs and was produced in a range
of vibrant, nonfading colors.

Plastic, American, ca. 1930s–1940s

The convincingly succulent vegetables and fruits pictured here are almost certainly from the "Style-Fruit" line of carved buttons and jewelry first introduced by Catalin in the thirties. Early in the decade the Catalin Corporation captured the plastics industry by introducing a new product, chemically similar to Bakelite, but which could be produced in over two hundred dazzling opaque, marbleized, translucent, and transparent colors. The apple and pear halves were designed by Marion Weeber in the 1940s for B. Blumenthal and Company.

Plastic, wood, and metal, chiefly American, ca. 1935–1960

The term "goofies" was coined in a 1942 button journal to describe the unconventional designs and shapes that were then being made from modern plastics and other materials. Buttons made in the shapes of the objects they represent, also known more literally as "realistics," enjoyed a tremendous vogue in the 1930s and 1940s, when button manufacturers vied for an increasingly demanding and rapidly changing market by producing ever more novel designs. Realistics were often carded and sold in sets of either identical or assorted buttons. Although inkwells and blackboards may no longer conjure up visions of high fashion, buttons like these were often created for a highly fashion-conscious adult market.

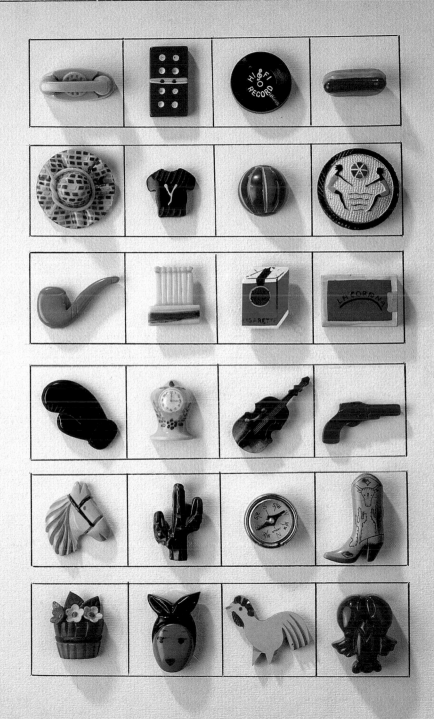

*Various materials and countries,
mid-20th century*

These hexagonal buttons are not only convincing depictions of dice, but striking abstract patterns as well. The group here employs a variety of materials, including, from top to bottom, bone, Bakelite, glass, enamel, and Bakelite again.

(opposite)
Paper, American, after 1941

It is not surprising that a period in which smoking in America was openly advertised for everything from diet to nerve control would produce buttons in paper and cardboard miniature reproductions of cigarette boxes. Buttons such as these were often sold in sets and can sometimes be dated according to the brand and style of the package. The Lucky Strike pack here indicates that the button was made after 1941, when "Lucky Strike Greens [went] to war," and the brand changed its wrapper to white.

Various materials, American, 20th century

From the end of the Civil War well into the twentieth century, largely demeaning images of blacks were depicted across a wide range of household objects and mass media. This small group of buttons embraces some of the most pervasive and deeply entrenched stereotypes: at top, a bone underwear button, transformed into an "Aunt Jemima," with buttonholes for eyes; below, two bug-eyed faces reminiscent of black-face masks and minstrel shows; at bottom, a fabric button, probably a depiction of "Topsy" from *Uncle Tom's Cabin,* a popular figure for dolls in the early 1930s. The painted Bakelite button at right portrays a distinct, but related vision—the uncivilized "native."

(opposite)
Plastic, French, ca. 1930–1940

These humorously suggestive buttons with shapely women and bright, primary colors, are hand-painted on white plastic. They were no doubt meant to appeal to a taste for the prurient and exotic.

Wood, American, ca. 1960s–1970s

The folkloric quality of the images on these American studio buttons by George E. Schmidt of Philadelphia, who worked in the 1960s and 1970s, is immediately apparent. Although the hand-carving appears simple, the designs are built up of several small pieces of assorted woods on a background of contrasting color, which is then set into the center of a wooden disk.

(opposite)
Fabric, American, probably 1st half of 20th century

Both the comforting slogans and the safe construction suggest that these fabric-covered, machine-stitched buttons were worn on a child's sleeper. Although these buttons probably date from the first half of the twentieth century, techniques for covering buttons by machine were employed in the United States from the mid-nineteenth century on. (enlarged)

Wood, American, mid-20th century

Intarsia and marquetry are both forms of veneer decoration in which designs are made from various pieces of wood placed side by side. These studio buttons combine inlay (intarsia) with applied veneer (marquetry) in white holly, walnut, cherry, and other indigenous woods. The highly polished and dramatic geometric patterns exploit the subtle graphic qualities of the wood itself. (enlarged)

Glossary

ajouré: pierced, perforated, or decorated with an openwork pattern

appliqué: designs created by affixing one material to the base of another

basse-taille: transparent or translucent enamel applied over a ground that has been chased, stamped, or carved in low relief; and, in later examples, engine-turned

bisque: unglazed white porcelain (*also called* "biscuit")

champlevé: enamel poured into grooves carved into metal and then polished down to the same level as the metal surface

cloisonné: enamel poured into compartments formed by metal bands on the surface of an object; the bands are raised or visible above the enamel surface

counterenamel: to enamel on the reverse side

crackle glaze: cracks made deliberately for decorative effect in a glazed surface

cut steel: steel cut as studs, faceted, polished, and riveted to a base, to provide brilliance

découpage: cutouts, usually of paper, applied to a surface and then covered with several layers of coating, usually lacquer or varnish

églomisé: (*see* verre églomisé)

émaux peints: polychrome painting on enamel

flint glass: glass made with silica from English flint

Florentine work: (*see* pietra dura)

foil: thin sheets of metal used as backgrounds to create color and brilliance; also small shapes of gold, silver, or enamel, called "paillons," used in translucent enameling

goofies: (*see* realistics)

grisaille: monochrome-painted enamel, usually shades of gray on white ground; also, a dark base of enamel, with varying thicknesses of white, producing a cameo effect

guilloché: enameling process in which transparent or translucent enamel is applied to a metal surface that has been engraved (originally by a "tour à guillocher," a machine capable of engraving metal in a variety of patterns)

habitat: button collectors' term for eighteenth-century French under-glass buttons containing plant and insect specimens

intarsia: inlay, especially of wood and usually pictorial (*cf.* marquetry)

jasperware: hard stoneware, pure white but often stained, most often cobalt blue, perfected by Wedgwood in the late eighteenth century

jet: compact black mineral, formed by pressure, heat, and chemical action, used to make jewelry in the late nineteenth century; black-glass buttons are often erroneously called "jet"

kagagami-buta: centerpiece of round netsukes (*cf.* manjū)

lacy glass: pressed glass with intricate relief patterns

manjū: circular netsuke made from carved wood, ivory, or horn, worn over man's obi sash as a counterweight for a purse or tobacco case (*cf.* kagagami-buta)

marcasite: crystalized iron pyrites, resembling cut steel in shape, but differentiated as they are hand-set rather than riveted to a base

marquetry: decorative veneer made of wood, shell, ivory, bone, etc. applied over a wood surface to form geometric or pictorial patterns (*cf.* intarsia)

micromosaic: mosaic of tiny fragments of colored glass (called "tesserae"), invented by Giacomo Raffaelli and developed in the Vatican workshops toward the end of the eighteenth century

passementerie: trimming of silver and gold threads often interwoven with sequins, pearls, paste, and other glittering materials

pâte-sur-pâte: method of decorating porcelain in relief in which designs are painted on successive coats of slip applied to unfired clay, practiced especially at Sèvres in France and Minton in England

picture buttons: collectors' term for buttons with pictorial subjects, usually metal, popular in the late nineteenth to early twentieth century

pietra dura: literally "hard stone," refers to the type of mosaic produced in Florence from the Renaissance to the present (*also called* "Florentine work")

piqué: process in which tortoiseshell or ivory is heated and then inlaid with silver or gold (in piqué point small gold or silver studs are inlaid, while in piqué posé silver or gold strips are inlaid)

plique-à-jour: enamel poured into compartments as in cloisonné but without a metal backing, thus allowing light to pass through the colored enamel

realistics: buttons made of various materials, particularly plastic, in realistic shapes (*also called* "goofies" by collectors)

repoussé: relief decoration on metalwork created by hammering from the underside

reverse painting: painting on the reverse side of glass so the finished work can be seen from the front

Rockingham ware: a mottled brown pottery glaze originated in England

rose-cut: method of gemstone cutting with a flat base and a number of triangular facets rising to a point

sand-cast: cast in a mold made of sand, particularly silver work by American Indians

Satsuma ware: Japanese crackle-glazed earthenware, finely painted and gilded

shakudo: the art of Japanese metalwork, using inlays of gold, copper, and silver, especially in sword making

Shibayama: a style of ivory inlay, using semiprecious stones and shell, named after an eighteenth-century Japanese carver of netsuke

strass: brilliant paste made of lead glass, used to simulate various transparent gemstones

tessera, tesserae: (*see* micromosaic)

transfer printing: process of decorating enamel or porcelain in which a copperplate is engraved and inked with ceramic colors and a print is made on paper that is then pressed onto the object

underglass: eighteenth-century button that has a thin layer of glass over a decorative surface, mounted in a metal frame

verre églomisé: glass painted in reverse with gold or silver leaf, or paint, then engraved with a fine needle

Wemyss ware: pottery decorated with bold underglaze paintings, made by the Fife Pottery of Robert Heron & Son, Kirkcaldy, Scotland, from 1883 to 1930

Selected bibliography

Decorative arts:

Arts, P. L. W. *Japanese Porcelain: A Collector's Guide to General Aspects and Decorative Motifs.* Lochem, The Netherlands: Tijdstrom, 1983.

Arwas, Victor. *The Liberty Style.* New York: Rizzoli, 1979.

Atterbury, Paul, ed. *The History of Porcelain.* New York: Morrow, 1982.

Becker, Vivienne. *Antique and Twentieth Century Jewellery.* London: N.A.G. Press, Ltd., 1980.

Blair, Claude, ed. *The History of Silver.* New York: Ballentine, 1987.

Davidov, Corinne, and Ginny Redington Dawes. *The Bakelite Jewelry Book.* New York: Abbeville Press, 1988.

DiNoto, Andrea. *Art Plastic: Designed for Living.* New York: Abbeville Press, 1984.

Ettesvold, Paul M. *The Eighteenth-Century Woman.* Exhibition catalogue. New York: The Metropolitan Museum of Art, 1981.

Fleming, John, and Hugh Honour. *The Penguin Dictionary of Decorative Arts.* London: Viking, 1989 (revised edition).

Groer, Leon de. *Decorative Arts in Europe, 1790–1850.* New York: Rizzoli, 1986.

Kelley, Lyngerda, and Nancy Schiffer. *Plastic Jewelry.* West Chester, Pennsylvania: Schiffer Publishing Ltd., 1987.

Lewis, M. D. S. *Antique Paste Jewelry.* London: Faber & Faber, 1970.

Liberty's, 1875–1975: An Exhibition to Mark the Firm's Centenary. Exhibition catalogue. London: Victoria and Albert Museum, 1975.

Maeder, Edward, ed. *An Elegant Art: Fashion and Fantasy in the Eighteenth Century.* Los Angeles and New York: Los Angeles County Museum of Art in association with Harry N. Abrams, 1983.

Newman, Harold. *An Illustrated Dictionary of Jewelry.* London: Thames and Hudson Ltd., 1981.

Phillips, Phoebe, ed. *The Encyclopedia of Glass.* New York: Crown, 1981.

Poynder, Michael. *The Price Guide to Jewellery.* Woodbridge, Suffolk, England: Baron, 1976.

Ramond, Pierre. *Marquetry.* Trans. Jacqueline Derenne. Newton, Conn.: Taunton Press, 1989.

Scarisbrick, Diana, et al. *Jewellery Makers, Motifs, History, Techniques.* London: Thames and Hudson Ltd., 1989.

Silverman, Debora L. *Art Nouveau in Fin-de-Siècle France: Politics, Psychology, and Style.* Berkeley: University of California Press, 1989.

Weisberg, Gabriel P., et al. *Japonisme: Japanese Influence on French Art, 1854–1910.* Cleveland: Cleveland Museum of Art, 1975.

BUTTONS:

Buttons in the Collection of the Cooper-Hewitt Museum. Washington, D.C.: The Smithsonian Institution, 1982.

Epstein, Diana. *A Collector's Guide to Buttons.* New York: Walker & Co., 1968.

Ertell, Viviane Beck. *The Colorful World of Buttons.* Princeton, J.J.: The Pyne Press, 1973.

Gandouet, Thérèse. *Boutons.* Paris: Les Editions de l'Amateur, 1984.

Ginsberg, Madeline. "Buttons: Art and Industry." *Apollo,* Vol. CV, No. 184 (June 1977), pp. 462–67.

Houart, Victor. *Buttons: A Collector's Guide.* New York: Charles Scribner Sons, 1977.

Hughes, Elizabeth, and Marion Lester. *The Big Book of Buttons.* Pennsylvania: Boyertown Publishing Co., 1981.

Just Buttons: Magazine for Button Collectors. October 1942–November/December 1979.

Luscomb, Sally C. *The Collector's Encyclopedia of Buttons.* New York: Crown, 1967.

National Button Bulletin, 1947 to present (1942–1946 titled: *National Button Society Quarterly Bulletin*)

A Note on Button Collections:

Still intact and on view in its original home is the Baroness Edmond de Rothschild's superb collection at Waddesdon Manor, in Buckinghamshire, England. In Paris, the renowned M. H. R. d'Allemagne Collection was sold, after d'Allemagne's death, to an American collector. It is documented in d'Allemagne's three-volume work *Les Accessoires du costume et du mobilier,* an early and invaluable reference for fine buttons. The Musée de la Mode et du Costume, in Paris, features eighteenth-century buttons; and in England, there are buttons in the Victoria and Albert Museum in London and in the Luckrock Collection at the Museum and Art Gallery of Birmingham.

In the United States, there are three notable button collections held by museums. In New York City, the Cooper-Hewitt National Museum of Design maintains an extensive international collection of buttons, representing most major styles and documenting materials and techniques of button design and manufacture. This collection was begun by Sarah and Eleanor Hewitt, founders of the Museum, and has been supplemented by donations over the decades; it is available for study by appointment. The Metropolitan Museum of Art has the Hanna Sicher Kohn Collection, and the extensive collection of Margaret Strong, an heiress of the Kodak fortune, is in the Strong Museum in Rochester, New York.

INDEX

Italic page numbers refer to captions and illustrations.